PCN Tours

A Companion to the Popular Television Series

Brian Lockman

Camino Books, Inc.
Philadelphia

Manufactured in the United States of America

1 2 3 4 5   05 04 03

ISBN 0-940159-68-6 (trade paperback)
ISBN 0-940159-81-3 (hardcover)

Library of Congress Cataloging-in-Publication Data

Lockman, Brian.
    PCN Tours : a companion to the popular television series / Brian Lockman.
        p.   cm.
    ISBN 0-940159-68-6 (trade paperback : acid-free paper)
  1. Industrial tours—Pennsylvania—Handbooks, manuals, etc. 2. Pennsylvania—Tours—Handbooks, manuals, etc. I. Pennsylvania Cable Network. II. Title.
    T49.5 .L63 2002
    670'.9748—dc21
                                    2002001806

Cover design: Debra Kohr Sheppard
Interior design: Jerilyn Kauffman

This book is available at a special discount on bulk purchases for promotional, business, and educational use. For information write to:

Publisher
Camino Books, Inc.
P.O. Box 59026
Philadelphia, PA 19102

www.caminobooks.com

Contents

Introduction

This is a book about a television program. The program, *PCN Tours*, is a weekly series that features tours of Pennsylvania's factories, museums, and historic sites. It is seen on Sunday nights on the Pennsylvania Cable Network, a nonprofit public affairs network serving cable television subscribers across the state.

Beginning in April 1995 with a tour of the Harley-Davidson plant in York, PA, *PCN Tours* has gathered a devoted following. While the vast majority of PCN's programming hours are devoted to coverage of Pennsylvania House and Senate floor debates, hearings, press conferences, call-in programs, and public policy events, PCN staff traveling throughout the state invariably meet with people who want to talk about nothing but "the tours." And their favorites are always the manufacturing tours.

Although every issue of *Time* or *Newsweek* features articles touting the "Information Age" or the "Internet Age," there is still a lot of *stuff* being made in Pennsylvania. And from what we hear from viewers, they love the opportunity to watch that stuff being made.

Originally seen as a weekly program and now as a daily, *PCN Tours* takes an approach rarely taken by television. That is, we keep our mouths shut. Every PCN tour is conducted by a spokesperson from the company being featured, often by supervisors who started out building the product with their own hands. No PCN-added narrator could ever convey the enthusiasm and pride exuded by, for example, the supervisor of the assembly line at Mack Trucks, Inc., in the Lehigh Valley. He loves his plant, and he loves his trucks. Or the president of York Barbell, who *knows* that his product is the best and *knows* that his workers are the best.

The popularity of *PCN Tours* has led to this book. The words you will read are the words of each tour guide, edited for length and clarity. The pictures are taken directly from the videotape of the televised tours. As with the television program, we keep our mouths shut and let the companies tell their own stories.

This book concentrates on 28 of PCN's factory tours, which give a small sample of the wide range of stuff still being made in Pennsylvania.

Acknowledgments

This book would never have been made if it first had not been a popular television program. Credit for the success of *PCN Tours* belongs to those people responsible for producing the program each week. Larry Kaspar, senior producer, designed the format and single-handedly produced, shot, and edited the first 150 tours. He has the job of trying to explain to companies just why they should let us take a camera into their factories. Corey Clarke and Josh Mackley now share shooting and editing duties with Larry. Like him, they must make each company's spokesperson comfortable in front of the camera. Like him, they have to plan and execute each tour on the fly with very little room for error.

Debra Kohr Sheppard, vice president of operations, oversaw the enormous project of identifying, capturing, cropping, and storing the hundreds of pictures that appear in this book. She was assisted by David Emenheiser, Robert Krout, Kevin Love, and Jolene Risser, who spent many hours converting the pictures from the original videotapes into computer files.

Pam Wert, PCN's manager of administration, while recuperating from surgery, took on the task of transcribing nearly all of the 28 tours included in this book. The work required many hours of patience and persistence, as well as a good ear. In addition, she made repeat phone calls to the subjects of this book to gather background information and verify facts.

Credit is due, also, to the rest of the staff at PCN, people who each day produce some of the most original and significant programming to appear on television anywhere. Their enthusiasm for this nonprofit network makes working there a joy. In addition to those named above, they are Brad Hammer, senior vice president; Bill Bova, vice president of programming; producers Theresa Elliott and Joe Qualtieri; engineers John Fox and Mark Kendall; master control operators Francine Cesari, Mick Corman, Nate Kresge, Jennifer Rogers, and Molly Sweigert; and promotions assistant Beth Ann McCoy.

Special thanks go to Nancy Karvois Lockman, my wife of 28 years. She was patient with me throughout this entire process and donated her time and expertise to the proofreading of this book. And thanks to my parents, Felix and Louise Lockman, for instilling in me a love of books and of reading, and to my daughters, Kimberly and Kathleen, who seem to have inherited the same trait.

Thank you to Pennsylvania's cable television companies, who created the Pennsylvania Cable Network as a nonprofit public service in 1979, and have shown good citizenship and community spirit by giving it their unwavering support for so many years. PCN is governed by a board of directors made up of representatives of the Pennsylvania cable television industry. They are: Chairman of the Board Donald G. Reinhard of Pencor Services, Inc.; Peter P. Brubaker, Susquehanna Media Company; James J. Duratz, Barco-Duratz Foundation; Joseph S. Gans, Gans Multimedia Partnership; Michael Rigas, Adelphia Communications Corporation;

William C. Stewart, The Armstrong Group of Companies; Robert J. Tarlton, one of cable television's earliest pioneers; and Hoyt D. Walter, Service Electric Cablevision.

And finally, thanks to two very special people who should be remembered. They are Yolanda G. Barco and her sister, Helene Barco Duratz, of Meadville, PA, both of whom passed away recently. For more than 20 years they were tirelessly dedicated to the Pennsylvania Cable Network and its public service mission. It is largely through their support, their efforts, and their belief in the value of this nonprofit company that PCN was able to survive its early years and grow into the statewide network it is today. We owe them a tremendous debt of gratitude. Pennsylvania is a better place because of them.

Brian Lockman

Foreword

"Do you think people will be interested in this?"

That's the question I heard while studying an exhibit on the wall of the Zippo lighter factory in Bradford, PA.

While preparing to host an installment of *PCN Tours*, a tour guide has often asked that question. If there is one thing that worries people to the point of acute self-consciousness, it's the prospect of exposing to the world something they do that will be boring. The answer was easy.

The wall display showed Zippo lighters, or more accurately, the *remains* of Zippo lighters, mounted as if they were insect specimens. A handwritten card appeared below each one explaining the demise of each lighter. One lighter had its hinged top nearly ripped in two. The card told all: "Bullet."

Another lighter had been blown to bits by some awesome force that rendered it unrecognizable. The card made it clear: "Combine."

Many other lighters had similar concise epitaphs. But why should Zippo put together an exhibit that shows such a dramatic relationship between a lighter and its owner? All these damaged lighters had been returned to the factory by their owners for free repair or replacement.

"Do you think people will be interested in this?"

I paused. "Oh, yeah," I said. "I know our viewers will enjoy this. There's probably nothing like it anywhere else in the world."

It started in 1995 with a simple question. What would be the result if the Pennsylvania Cable Network visited a factory with a hand-held video camera and a wireless microphone and asked company officials to give us a tour of the place from raw materials to the packaged product? No complicated, tedious setup of lights, no makeup, no one running around with an instrument to measure light levels, and no television production crew of ten or more people. Just one person shooting video from the shoulder, using a small camera with a wide lens. Producer, director, sound engineer, cajoler, and commiserator, all in one. The camera would show what was being described, while recording the voice of the tour guide at the same time. We would keep the camera in motion and the tape rolling whenever possible. That would achieve two things: a "you-are-there" feeling for the viewer and a dramatic reduction in editing time. The latter was necessary in order to fit the demands of a weekly one-hour television program into all the other requirements of operating a 24-hour-a-day public affairs television network.

A few years and a couple of hundred programs later, *PCN Tours* is without a doubt the most recognized offering on our network. What can explain the popularity of this humble program? Maybe there is a sense of adventure or suspense about what we are going to see after we round the next corner. Maybe viewers like the video vérité technique. Perhaps our down-to-earth tour guides are the attraction. What is the thread that runs through all our tour programs that seems to make them a consistently rewarding viewing experience? I think it has less to do with tangible things and more to do with human nature. People enjoy seeing *stuff* put together. Everybody likes the idea of building or creating. Maybe viewers get a vicarious kick out of seeing something recognizable evolve from raw materials, as though they had a hand in it.

The companies we feature do not hire actors with reassuring voices to be their spokespersons. The brave souls who take on the challenge of leading *PCN Tours* are not professional performers. They are experts on their companies. Usually our tour guides are in charge of production at their factories and represent the best-qualified persons to explain how their products are made. They know their workers' names. Each guide shares an infectious love for the company and pride in its craftsmanship and products.

From its home in Bradford, PA, Zippo takes great pride in honoring the terms of its warranty. As we visit other companies, pride often emerges as a motivating force for managers and employees alike.

In an age when much manufacturing goes overseas in search of cheaper labor and materials, the following pages show that companies, some with well-known reputations and some whose names have become part of our national lexicon, are still making things right under our noses here in Pennsylvania.

Larry Kaspar
Senior Producer, *PCN Tours*

Location	Allen Organ Company
	150 Locust Street
	Macungie, PA 18062
	(610) 966-2202
	www.allenorgan.com
Hours	Public tours available by appointment.
	Museum open daily, 8:00 a.m. to 4:30 p.m.,
	or by appointment if after hours.
Tour Guide	Barry Holben
	Vice President of Sales

Welcome to the largest organ-building facility in the world, here at Macungie, PA. Before we go to our factory, I'd like to spend a few minutes telling you about the Allen Organ Company's history and show you the evolution of our technology and how we came to be the world's largest organ builder. (1)

The Allen Organ Company was founded by Jerome Markowitz, who wanted to find a way to use twentieth-century technology to make a pipe-organ sound. In the early 1930s, when Jerome decided to find a new way to build organs, he concentrated on electronic components instead of pipes. The tone generation racks he built for his very first organ were huge racks of components that were actually radio surplus gear. This is all that remains of that first organ. ②

By the late 1950s and early 1960s, the tone generation medium had moved from vacuum tubes to transistors. Transistors were invented by the Bell Labs only about 10 miles from our facilities. And these small, silver, cylindrical components are the transistors, which by this time had replaced vacuum tubes in our tone generation. The whole tone generation for the organ was on a board this size. ③

Both the solid-state components and the earlier vacuum tubes were analog. The organs at that time contained electronic circuits, which would oscillate at different frequencies. The engineers would try to adapt the characteristics of those circuits so that the sound they produced was pipelike. But it really was just an imitation of what happened in the pipes, not the sound of pipes themselves.

It wasn't until a breakthrough in technology in the late 1960s that we were able to change the way we make the sound, from an imitation of the pipes to an actual duplication of the sound of pipes themselves. And oddly enough, it took the Apollo space program to provide us with the technology.

In the late 1960s, North American Rockwell was developing the microcircuits that eventually fueled the whole computer revolution. And they needed these circuits to design a small computer, which could go on board the Apollo spacecraft and calculate its re-entry pattern. After that development, the company looked for ways to use that technology commercially, and in a joint effort with the Allen Organ Company, North American Rockwell and Allen developed the world's first musical instrument that utilized digital technology.

What made digital technology so different from the analog technology our company had used before is that instead of just imitating the sound of a pipe using electronic circuits, digital technology took a picture of the sound much the same way that CDs today record sound digitally. The numbers, which represented the computer picture of the sound, were stored inside the computer's memory. And when the organ was played, they were used to recreate the sound in a sort of connect-the-dots pattern to reassemble the original wave shape of the pipe sound.

The amazing thing about technology at that time was that all of the circuitry used for tone generation was now shrunk into an area smaller than my fingernail. This chip contains approximately 3,000 transistors. ④ Each of those transistors was a memory location for storing information about sound. These tiny microcircuits were then mounted on larger circuit boards, and this became the tone generation for the world's first digital musical instruments.

Now, as remarkable as it seems to be able to put 3,000 transistors in a tiny area like this, today we are able to put about 32 million transistors in the same area. And the reason it's so important to have this many transistors or memory locations in an instrument is because just like any other computing device, the more memory you have, the more detail you can store about the original event. In this case, the details that we're storing are of pipe-organ sound, and that's why our instruments today are able to store such realistic sound, and why our instruments sound like pipe organs.

To show you how we record the sounds that we put in the organs, we've come to a very unusual room here in the development section of our factory. This room is called an anechoic chamber. ⑤ It's a room that is designed to be without echoes.

I'm standing on a metal grid that's suspended above huge wedges of fiberglass. Even the foundation of the floor floats so that subterranean sound waves from trucks and other vehicles passing by our factory can't be picked up. It's in this very acoustically pure environment that we record the pipes, and these recordings are used for the sounds that our instruments play. We've got a few pipes set up here, and the microphone that's positioned here in front of the pipes is attached to a computer in the next room. The sound is digitally recorded by this microphone and used later in the computer storage of the actual instruments.

Within our electronic assembly area we have many different ways of automating and speeding up this manufacturing process. This machine contains raw circuit boards and the components that are necessary to go onto those boards. The whole machine is operated by a computer control system. The machine inserts individual components through the holes in the circuit board and clips off the other end for the soldering process. ⑥

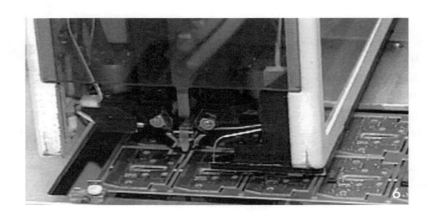

When the machine has finished its work, the components are mounted on the circuit board, and on the opposite side the individual pins that connect the component to the board have been crimped over and are ready to be soldered. ⑦ Years ago, this process would have been done by hand, and someone with a soldering iron would have had to individually solder each connection. On a small board there may be only 30 or 40 connections, but on a large board there can be hundreds of them. To make that process more efficient, we've automated the soldering as well.

An Allen organ was used during the premiere performance of Leonard Bernstein's *Mass* at the opening of the Kennedy Center in 1971.

The board that we have been talking about is a component mounting technique called through-hole. The components' individual leads go through holes in the circuit board, and on the reverse side those leads are soldered to the holes in the circuit board, making the connection with all the traces on the board. This was a great technique years ago. But today technology has allowed the components to shrink in size to be these tiny little dots that you see on the paper. ⑧ These rec-

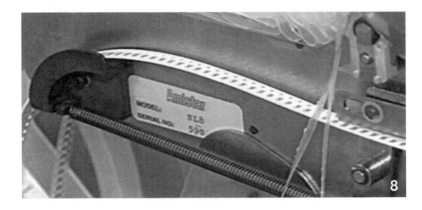

The world's largest digital instrument is an Allen organ at the Bellevue Baptist Church of Cordova, TN. The organ employs more than 250 speaker cabinets located in seven chambers throughout the 7,000-seat Worship Center.

tangular areas are actually individual components for circuit boards, and using the types of machines that we've seen so far, to apply them to the circuit boards would be impossible. The wires that come out of these individual components are so small, you often need a microscope or a magnifying glass to see them. So it was necessary to invent a new process of affixing them to the circuit board. The process is called surface mount. Instead of going through holes on the circuit board, the components are mounted on the surface with a kind of paste. We use a machine to apply the paste to circuit boards. Even the application of paste is so sensitive that it's necessary to have a computer system for that purpose.

After all the components are mounted, the board continues on its way through the conveyor into an oven, which will cure the paste and permanently affix all the components as they need to be for operation.

Here you see an amplifier being assembled. (9) These amplifiers, when they are completed, produce 100 watts per channel RMS [root mean square], and as many as four channels per amplifier module. We even build the sheet metal components for these amplifiers in-house. At this station the transformer and the power capacitors are being mounted inside the amplifier. And even the transformer for this amplifier is built in-house. After the capacitors and transformers and controls are mounted, the individual amplifier modules are inserted into a cage.

We use modular design throughout our instruments. Every component or every major subassembly is fitted with plugs, so that if service becomes necessary in the field, it's simply a matter of unplugging the faulty assembly or component and replacing it with a new one from the service kit. There's no necessity for soldering in the field.

Of course, the electronic components of our instruments are housed inside wooden consoles. In the carpentry shop of our factory, the wood comes in rough-cut, rough-sawn pieces like these, and by the time it leaves, it's a finished console. (10) We work primarily in oak and American walnut. After the stock has been

milled and cut to size, it's cut into its final shape. That process is accomplished by the use of automated routers, which are computer-controlled, and can automatically cut parts to precise dimensions.

As with any fine furniture, we do bookend matching on the grains of the console panels so that if you look at the grain on one side of the console, you'll see that it matches perfectly to the grain on the other side. You'll also notice by looking at a cross section of this console that we use fine butcher block construction on the console components and real hardwood veneers. These consoles are built with the same quality that you'd expect to find in the finest furniture you could purchase for your home. ⑪

An Allen organ was installed in Rome's Sistine Choir School in 1982.

After our consoles are assembled, they're brought to our sanding department, where they're sanded by hand. After the consoles have been sanded, they are brought to the finishing department, where stain and lacquer are applied. There are a number of other components on the instruments that need to be finished: pedals, speaker assemblies, and the consoles themselves. We can even finish a console to match existing woodwork in the customer's sanctuary. If a church sends us a pew or a hymn rack from the church, we can custom-finish the instrument to match perfectly. ⑫

A finished console has to be more than a beautiful piece of furniture, however. It's the control center, which the musician uses to play the music. To do that he needs the keyboard. The keyboards we use for our organs are manufactured in-house. They feature real-wood sticks to which plastic or wood or other material is affixed as a key surface. Each key has its own adjusting mechanism, which limits not only the travel but the tension of the keys as well. Here, each of our keyboards is adjusted by hand both for the contact point of individual keys and for the tension of the key itself. ⑬

At the end of each key stick on a circuit board you see a tiny tube of glass inside of which are two very small pieces of metal. ⑭ These metal pieces are drawn together by a magnet on the end of the key stick. As the key is depressed, the magnet comes closer to these two pieces of metal inside the tube, and they make contact. The tube itself is filled with inert gas so that the atmosphere in which the metal contacts are placed can never corrode or allow dirt and pollution from the environment to get on the contact. This is an excellent method to make sure these keyboards work in dirty or dusty environments for long periods of time. We developed this method, and it has proven to be virtually problem-free in the field.

These finished keyboard assemblies will be used in a large floor manual instrument and feature another method of contact actuation, which we developed in-

house. This system allows the keys to be velocity-sensitive. That means that if the organ is set to sound like a piano, you can control the touch of the keys by the velocity of the keys, as you would on an acoustic instrument. In order to determine the velocity of the key, we've placed an infrared sensor on either side of a small metal vein at the back of the key stick. As this metal vein bisects the beam of infrared light, a computer attached to the circuit board computes the amount of time in milliseconds it's taken to go from maximum beam amplitude to zero. It converts that amount of time into a discrete velocity. (15)

This is the final stop in the assembly of our instrument. At this stage the instrument looks complete from the outside, but still needs to have all of its components assembled inside. Instead of using an assembly line, we use a process whereby each console is assigned to one worker who assembles all of the components inside and does all of the wiring. If you look up and down the line, we have a number of different instruments being assembled, all shapes and sizes. They are all assembled using the same method and all with the same quality of components. (16)

After the instruments are completed, they're brought here to the stock area, where each one of them awaits its turn in one of our final checkout rooms. After the instrument is completed, it's attached to the speakers with which it will be shipped, and sent through a rigorous procedure, testing of all its functions, both musical and mechanical. The technician here makes sure that every stop works correctly, that all of the computer functions built into the console work correctly, and that it sounds good before it leaves our factory. (17)

Tour 2

Location	Boeing
	Route 291 and Stewart Avenue
	Ridley Park, PA 19078
	(610) 591-2700
	www.boeing.com
Hours	No public tours available.
Tour Guide	Sebastian J. Arrigo
	Chinook Operations Manager

What we're going to do today is go through our manufacturing facility and look at some of our products. The first one we'll see is the CH-47 Chinook, which we build in its entirety, flight test, and deliver. Then we're going to look at the V-22, which we build in conjunction with our partner Bell Helicopter in Fort Worth, TX. And we'll also touch on what we call our Commercial Airplane Support Activities, where we build sections for the wing of the 767 and 777. We ship those to Seattle, where they are installed in the major commercial aircraft.

We're going to start with the CH-47 Chinook. ① We build the helicopter in four major sections. When we get to final assembly, we bring them all together and we splice them. As we move down the final assembly line, we install components,

hydraulic tubes, wiring, transmissions, and engines. We do functional tests to make sure that everything operates correctly, and then we move the aircraft to flight test. And after it's acceptable to us, we deliver it to the customer.

What you see here is a partially completed floor section, which we build on its side. ② It's easier to assemble and seal that way. Eventually this will rotate down,

we'll add the skins and the roof crown, and make a completed cabin section. The box in the center is the area for the cargo hook. The CH-47 can carry up to 28,000 pounds. So the hook is essential for lifting huge loads. But this is a traditional web and stringer assembly with machine floor beam frames, web, and skin. It's sealed to keep out water, because the CH-47 can also land on water and operate almost like a boat.

We have a number of jigs and stations where we do our major assembly. This is the cockpit assembly tool. We bolt it together with many fasteners around the side, and seal it. This is the cockpit section looking forward; that is, the front of the helicopter looking out of the windshield. The final shape of the aircraft will be much clearer as we get to the other portions of final assembly. ③

This is the aft section. This opening in the back will eventually have a ramp. The ramp comes up and down to allow troops to come in and out. It also allows loading for cargo. You can drive a jeep or a small automobile or cargo litters on a roller system. ④

Here's our aft pylon. A transmission will sit in the top, and it will contain the rotor head. ⑤

Next we're going to go to the final assembly, where we splice the sections of the aircraft together. We add the ramp and we add the transmissions, attach the landing gear, and attach the external fuel tanks.

This is the start of our final assembly area, where we put the aircraft into the loading jigs. Here we have a staging area for a number of the components that we

The company traces its lineage to 1940, when Frank Piasecki and Harold Venzi, two engineering students at the University of Pennsylvania, established the P-V Engineering Forum and began designing and building rotary-wing aircraft. The company's first aircraft, the single-seat PV-2, completed its first flight in 1943, the second helicopter to fly in the United States.

The Boeing CH-47 Chinook is not only used to move troops, but also flies missions that include medical evacuation, aircraft recovery, fire fighting, parachute drops, heavy construction, civil development, disaster relief, and search and rescue.

need to install. What you see here is our aft main landing gear. ⑥ We buy these from a supplier. Also in this area we have long-range fuel pods that get attached to the outside of the helicopter as our primary fuel containment system. This helicopter contains five transmissions. A forward, an aft, a combiner, and left and right engine transmissions. So we have five transmissions to drive the two rotor systems.

We talked earlier about how we were going to bring the major sections together. That is done in this area. ⑦

Even prior to splicing, we start routing our wiring. After we wire this section, we will coil and stow the cables. And after the aircraft is spliced, we'll pull them through the lightening holes and all the way to the cockpit section.

What you see here is the next stage in final assembly. ⑧ We have a completely spliced aircraft, and we're finalizing our wiring and component installation. When that's done, we'll be

putting the ramp in. Our inspector reviews the attach points or installations to make sure they're in accordance with the drawing. When this is all completed, we move up to the next stage, where we'll run some functional tests. Eventually we'll put blankets up in the cabin section area, and you won't see all of that wiring.

We are now on top of the work stands. It's basically the second floor or the penthouse level, where we do our upper deck work in the pylons. ⑨ At this point

you can see the aft transmission, the combiner transmission. That combiner transmission takes the rotary forces of both engines, mixes them together, and goes through both transmissions.

Next we come to our last station in final assembly. This is when the aircraft has had everything installed, and all the functional items have been checked. The aircraft is now painted. One of the things that we do in this particular bay is simulate rain. The whole bay has overhead showerheads. We drop the curtains and then release the rain. We check all the sealing that we looked at earlier in the structural areas to make sure that the water does not get into the aircraft on essential equipment and personnel. ⑩

This is the aft section that we saw earlier. (11) There you can get a look at the blanket installation we talked about. Also to the left and the right are troop seats. Those are canvas litters that fold down much like a canvas lawn chair, and that's where the troops sit. This aircraft will hold upwards of 35 troops. This can also be the main cargo area if that is the particular need. Troop transport and cargo transport are the two major functions.

Of course, this aircraft contains a large number of different hardware, fasteners, grommets, nuts, bolts, and clamps. We keep our parts storage area very neat and very orderly. We do this to prevent foreign-object damage on the aircraft. Aircraft drive systems and engine systems are very sensitive to debris, particularly metal debris. We try to do an extremely good job of keeping loose items off the floor, and off the aircraft. It's very controlled as to who gets on the aircraft and what they have with them.

This is our flight test facility. (12) After the aircraft moves from the final rain position, which we just saw, it goes here. Our primary function here is to hang the blades,

put fuel in the aircraft, make sure we don't have any leaks, and check out all our systems. We also do our communication and navigation installations. Then we do a safety flight inspection, and prepare the aircraft for flight. We fly it to our satisfaction and to the customer's. We expect this whole process to take not more than 25 or 30 days. This particular aircraft is getting prepared for delivery. We have it opened up for inspection by the customer, prior to delivery to the United Kingdom for the RAF.

Another aspect of manufacturing takes place in this facility. As I said earlier, we do partial assemblies for Boeing Commercial in Seattle, WA. We build major wing sections for the 767 Outboard Leading Edge and the 777 Fixed Leading Edge. We build it to their design and manufacturing requirements, we put it on a truck and send it to Seattle, and they incorporate it into the Leading Edge.

Here we're looking at the 777 Fixed Leading Edge. We have design authority for this portion of the aircraft. We got the basic requirements of the aircraft, and we did the actual design. We then integrated it with their aircraft, and did it very successfully. That skin that you see there is composite skin. ⑬

The company moved to its present location in 1962, a 350-acre facility that now employs 5,400 people.

The Boeing Company is the world's largest manufacturer of commercial jetliners and military aircraft, and the nation's largest NASA contractor. In terms of sales, Boeing is the largest U.S. exporter.

The next product that we're going to look at is the V-22 Osprey, which is a tilt-rotor technology, meaning that it takes off like a helicopter, the rotors convert to an airplane configuration, then it flies like an airplane. It's very efficient, it's very fast, and has a much-extended range. It does not have the lift capacity that the CH-47 does. It has a little different technology in that it's primarily a composite structure, with composite frames and composite stiffeners. It is essentially built in the same fashion, and in primarily three sections: the aft empennage, the main cabin, and the cockpit. What we do here is complete the fuselage. We attach the landing gear and we stuff it with wiring, hydraulic tubing, and components. We do some functional testing, and then we ship the aircraft to Bell Textron in Fort Worth, TX. They complete the wing assembly, and then complete the flight testing in Patuxent River, MD.

On the following page you see the aft empennage. ⑭ We actually have two units here, which we're about to splice. This is all composite fiber skin and composite stiffeners. You don't see the same technology that you see in the CH-47, which has sheet-metal webs, metal formers and stiffeners, and metal fasteners. These are all baked-in composites.

This is the cockpit section for the same aircraft. ⑮   Here the wiring and installations are completed. The console and instrument panel frame installation is complete. The instruments haven't been installed yet. A lot of that gets done in Texas. But this is in its final preparation and very soon this piece will move over and mate with its other two components and complete the splice.

Here we see a fully spliced aircraft where all three sections are complete. ⑯ The cockpit, which we just looked at, the cabin, and the aft empennage make a complete assembly. Our customer for this one is the United States Navy.

That completes our tour of the main manufacturing facility. I say "the main facility" because, due to time constraints, we didn't look at our wire fabrication assembly. Across the street we have a very large composite center where we manufacture the rotor blades, which you saw, along with many of the composite skin panels for the commercial aircraft. At this facility, Boeing of Philadelphia, we have approximately 5,400 employees. We have a very bright outlook. We're very optimistic about our ability to sell and produce more aircraft here, and our goal is to be here for a

long, long time. I hope that occasionally, when you look up in the sky, you can see a CH-47 Chinook flying overhead. The Pennsylvania National Guard uses them, and the V-22 is used down in Patuxent River, MD. (17)

At the height of the Vietnam War, Boeing employed 14,000 people working three shifts. At one point the company was producing 30 Chinooks each month.

Throughout the 1940s and 1950s, the company operated as Piasecki Helicopter Corporation and then as Vertol Aircraft Corporation. The company was acquired by Boeing in 1960.

Location	Byers' Choice 4355 County Line Road Chalfont, PA 18914 (215) 822-6700 www.byerschoice.com
Hours	Public tours available Monday through Saturday, 10:00 a.m. to 5:00 p.m.; Sunday, 12:00 noon to 5:00 p.m. Museum open daily, same as tour hours.
Tour Guide	Bob Byers, Jr. President

Welcome to Byers' Choice, home of Byers' Choice carolers. We started a little over 25 years ago making the Byers' Choice carolers. They were first made by my mother around the kitchen table, and they've grown in popularity to the point where we employ about 180 artisans who manufacture these right here in Chalfont, PA. ①

Out on the production floor, all carolers start with a coat hanger. We cut the ends off the corners, and parts of it will be bent to form legs, the spine, and the arms. All of the parts of the coat hanger are bent in a jig, as you can see here. ② We have several different sizes of wire forms that match children, or adults, or teenagers, or figures that are moving like dancers or skaters.

We take the wire jigs that were just bent, and they will go to our plaster room. We'll mix the plaster and hand-spoon it onto the table, and then other artisans will follow behind and put in the wire jig. The plaster takes about 25 minutes to cure, at which point it's removed from the table and put into a laundry basket, where it will finish curing over the next week or so. ③

Also in this room we produce our plaster dogs and cats. When we pour plaster into the mold, it takes 25 minutes for it to cure. After it's cured, we'll remove the mold and pull it away from the plaster dog or cat, and you'll get an animal such as this. (4) We will then finish it off by scraping the bottom and carving out the eyes to make sure that it's ready for the next artisans in the production line. After the plaster has cured, the dogs and cats will come out to a work station where we will airbrush them. Each one is handpainted, and we probably do about 24 to 36 breeds of dogs and another 24 to 36 breeds of cats.

The first dogs and cats were designed by employees here at Byers' Choice. We had a store owner who asked for animals to go with the caroler family, and so my mother decided to have a contest among all of our employees. Quite a few of them sculpted various dogs and cats of different breeds. We all voted on which ones were the best, and the winner came into our line the following year. After the dogs and cats are airbrushed, the nose, the mouth, and other features are added to give life and color to the animal.

After the carolers' bases are painted, we then wrap the bodies out of tissue paper. We have different bodies for different figures. A man or woman, or a boy or girl, or teenagers, all have different-size bodies, but they're all made from tissue paper. Our wrappers take tissue paper and tape, and they sculpt the body from the various materials at their disposal. But just as no two human bodies are the same, no two wrapped bodies end up being the same. It's not uncommon that some people tend to wrap fatter bodies, and some people tend to wrap thinner bodies. It's just more reflective of different anatomical shapes in society as a whole. (5)

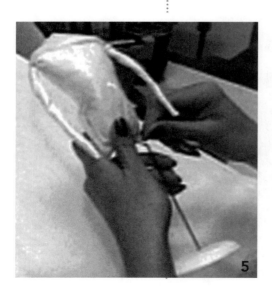

As the bodies are being made, we also are manufacturing heads. We have a special air-dry clay that has been developed for us, which is cut into predetermined amounts. Those pieces are then put into plaster molds. Each mold comes from a master that was created by my mother, Joyce Byers. She has sculpted several hundred heads, and we've made molds of each one. We'll put the clay in the molds and press the clay in. Then the molds will be taken back to an artisan workbench where the clay is removed. (6)

Each head is handcrafted in and of itself. So even though the clay will come out of the same mold, each one is different due to the process that takes place in pulling it out of the mold. The header releases the clay from the mold by moving it back and forth from the edges, and in doing so slightly distorts the clay and changes it. And each time the head is pulled out of a mold it gets distorted slightly differently. The artisans will then take the clay head and see what corrections need to be made, such as smoothing it out, adding any undercuts that are necessary, such as nostrils, or sometimes working around the chin. Then they will put it on a board to dry for a day. ⑦

> The company gives 20 percent of its profits each year to charitable organizations throughout the community. A large number of employees conduct food drives and help other local organizations.

> The company occupies a 75,000-square-foot facility and employs 180 people.

After the fleshing is completed, it will take a day to dry, and then we'll paint the features on the face. The artisans who work on the features will come by and paint in the eyes, cheeks, and lips. And the artisans decide what colors to use to add as much life and expression to the figure as possible. That helps give each figure a unique, handcrafted appearance. Each artisan in this department will do all three jobs, the heading, the fleshing, and the featuring, on all of their heads. So they are actually creating the head from start to finish. ⑧

8

All of the carolers are still designed by my mother. She made the first carolers as decorations for the Christmas table, and the relatives liked them so much that they received them the next year as gifts. Following that, they were sold in some consignment stores and proved so popular that they moved into retail stores and are now sold around the country in about 3,000 locations. But the costuming is still designed by my mother here at the factory. She will take a look at all the fabrics we have in inventory. At any given time we may have 300 different styles of tartan woolens, knits, velveteen, and cotton. And by mixing and matching whatever is on hand, she'll come up with the designs that fit the caroler look, which generally recalls Dickensian England.

Most of our cutting is done with table saws. As in much of the garment industry, we spread out layers of fabric on a table up to 40 feet long, and then we figure out the best way to take out all of the pieces that we're going to need to cut for the next eight weeks. We lay them out on the fabric, mark it with chalk, then cut the fab-

9

ric all at one time. The strips may be sewn into sleeves for the figures, or the rectangles will become something like a jacket, or they could be sewn into a hat. Because we're working on such a small scale, if you're off by just a little bit when you cut, it can make a huge difference. If you think of caroler-size clothes versus people's clothes, half an inch on a caroler translates to about three feet on people's clothes. So there are huge variations, and we need to be very accurate with everything we cut. ⑨

Now that we have our heads, our bodies, and our clothes, they all come together in our dressing department. Here we will sign the Byers' name to the back of each figure, and each figure will be numbered one of 100, two of 100, and so on. Then the socks or pants will be put on the figure. In this case we're looking at a little boy or girl, and socks and knickers are being added with pins and glue. The pins will be removed after the glue dries. ⑩

After the pants are put on a figure, the body will come here along with the head. Another dresser will add the jacket, the sleeves, the mittens, the head, the hat, and the hair. The dresser's job is to take the shapes and to conform them to the individual body to bring the character to life. They'll remove the pins from the pants after the glue is dry and add glue to the hands to hold the mittens in place.

This dresser is now working with the sleeves of the caroler. ⑪ She'll pull them on, and they'll be held in place by pins. Then the shirt will be placed on top. After

the vest is added, we'll put on the jacket, and everything is then tidied up to make sure it's draped properly and looks like actual clothing. The head will then be added to the top. It's glued in place, and then the collar is placed around the neck to hold it in place as well. All of our carolers wear hats because of our heading process. The backs of the heads are not finished, and that allows us to pull the figures directly out of the molds back in the heading department. As such, we can't have bald-headed men or women without hats, so the majority of figures are all wearing hats. The figures are also all singing, because the original carolers that we made were my mother's. When she thought of Christmas, her memories as a child were about singing and Christmas caroling. So her original figures were all singing with open mouths.

We've carried that tradition through on our figures to this day, and that is one of the things that gives the carolers their distinctive look. Every group of carolers is like a community of figures that have broken out in song. Now the dresser just adds the hair, the sideburns, and then the hat. And each figure gets a signature piece of holly to add a little bit of color. Each figure is then posed so it has some life and character. And if it has a specific accessory—in this case, the butler is bringing in the bucket of champagne to celebrate the holidays—that will be added as a finishing touch. ⑫

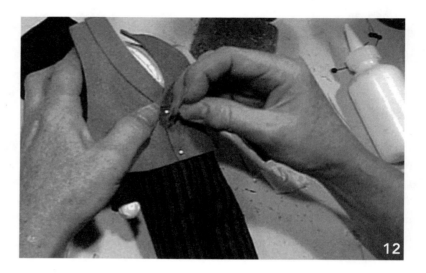

Byers' Choice is still a family-run business. It was started by my mother and father 22 years ago, when my mother hired her first employee to help her make carolers. She had been doing it all herself, sculpting heads by hand and dressing all the carolers herself. My father from the start handled the business side, working with sales and the banks. They have two sons, my brother and me. I came into the business about 10 years ago to help with production, and my brother, Jeff, handles sales and marketing for the firm. At Byers' Choice we try to create a light, airy, creative work environment. We have skylights throughout the building, we have art on the walls, and we do a lot of fun things to allow people to feel more at home and feel more creative, so their creativity can come out in the product itself. That's what brings the carolers to life, and it really shows. ⑬

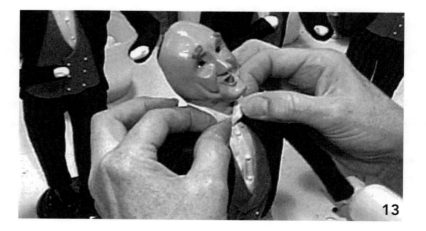

Chamberlain

Location	Chamberlain Manufacturing
	156 Cedar Avenue
	Scranton, PA 18505
	(570) 342-7801
	www.cmcscr.org
Hours	No public tours available.
Tour Guide	Bob Mitvalsky
	Vice President of Operations

Chamberlain Manufacturing is the operating contractor of the United States government's Scranton Army Ammunition Plant. We're a 15-acre facility. We have 500,000 square feet of manufacturing space. We are considered to be a full-service manufacturing facility in that we receive metal directly from the mills, we process it by sawing it, heating it, forging it, rough-machining it, heat-treating it, finish-machining it, and painting it. When it leaves here, it is a completed product. ①

In the billet yard, which you see on the following page, all of our incoming material is received either by tractor-trailer or by railcar, and is unloaded by two 25-ton overhead cranes. We receive our steel primarily from two mills in Ohio. The steel

is loaded on carts by fork truck, and the carts are pulled into our forging area, where we'll saw it and forge it. (2)

Our buildings were erected in the early 1900s and were originally used by the Erie-Lackawanna Railroad as a repair shop. In the early 1950s, the United States government took over the facility and made it into an artillery shell manufacturing plant. Chamberlain took over operation of the plant in 1963. (3)

The plant went through a very extensive modernization program in 1960, spending in excess of $100 million, in which we put in new forge lines and some new heat-treating furnaces, and automated a lot of our equipment. We have become very environmentally conscious. In 1996 alone we were given three awards. We were given the Federal Energy Management Award for our conservation efforts in energy, we received the Governor's Award for Waste Water Conservation, and we received an award from the United States Army Materiel Command for energy conservation.

Here you can see some of the products that we make at Chamberlain. ④ We've got the mortar family that we're producing now. We have been in the mortar program since 1991. The rate at which the plant produces mortars has varied from 7,000 per month to about 20,000 per month.

In 1997, the company produced its 20 millionth projectile, 14 million of which are the 155-millimeter projectiles.

In addition to its work for the military, Chamberlain offers forged steel products in final form to meet any customer standard and production rate.

Another product is the 5-inch projectile that we're making for the United States Navy that goes aboard their gunships. We are making the Navy projectile at a rate of anywhere from 7,000 to 10,000 a month.

Today we're going to follow one specific product we are making, which is a mortar. Our product breadth covers parts in sizes from about $3\frac{1}{2}$ to 4 inches in diameter up to 8 inches in diameter. We've run billets at weights of 4 pounds up to 200 pounds.

Here in the forge shop building we have six press lines. Press lines are made of either two or three presses in combination with mechanical hydraulic or all-hydraulic presses. The presses range in size from 400 tons up to 2,500 tons. The presses are serviced by either induction heating or gas-fired furnace. One of our older, more conventional ways of heating billets is through a gas-fired rotary hearth furnace. This furnace is capable of handling 20,000 pounds an hour. The billet is inserted into the hearth. ⑤ Then the hearth brings the billet up to a temperature of around 2,200 degrees. ⑥

On the following page you can see the base of the furnace, where we use a magnet to

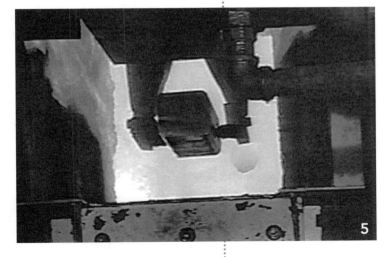

pick up a billet. ⑦ It pulls the billet back over to the loader, which takes it up to the mouth of the furnace. A robot arm that has water running through it to prevent overheating loads the billet into the rotary hearth furnace. The forge shop operates on a 16-hour day. We run two shifts of eight hours apiece. The reason for this is that once we get the furnace up to temperature, we want to keep it running for the week.

Next, the projectiles are loaded for the rough-turn operation. All of Chamberlain's rough-turn equipment has central coolants provided to it. We have an in-ground, 6,000-gallon central cooling system. All of the turnings from the machine operation go onto a conveyor and all the chips are conveyored to the back end of the shop, where they are crushed and loaded into a railcar for selling of scrap back to the steel mill. ⑧

The company was founded in 1906 in Waterloo, IA, as the Waterloo Rope Belt Company and was renamed Chamberlain Machine Works the following year. It has been at its present location since 1962.

The projectile that we have been following is the M804, or 155-millimeter mortar. This is a training round used by the Army. ⑨ You can see the projectile after it's been rough-turned; the back end has been faced off. And now we're at the accumulation table where we go into our next process, which is called hot-form nosing.

Whether we're running the 155-millimeter or the 120-millimeter, the process is identical. Today, we're nosing the 120-millimeter mortar. The 120-millimeter gets loaded on the conveyor and it goes through a series of washing operations where we wash off the machining oils and the machining coolants to clean the surface and get all the grit off of it. We put it through something like a big dishwasher. We wash it with hot, soapy water, and we rinse it and bring it up to a temperature of about 160 degrees.

In this operation the projectile has been rough-turned, it's been washed and cleaned, it's been heated, and it's had a graphite coating applied to it. It gets picked up by the robot, and stood up on end in the carousel. The carousel goes into an induction coil where we heat the projectile about 12 inches down from the base to about 1,400 to 1,600 degrees. You can see the hot projectile as it has been heated. From there the robot arm picks the projectile up and we hydraulically close the nose on it. ⑩

The important thing to understand about this operation is that as you close the nose, your ability to do anything else to the inside, other than paint it, has gone. You can't go in and do any other machining to it. So as that press closes the nose, the volume or the amount of product that projectile can hold is set. There's no changing it now. And with the military specifications for the projectile we have to control the volume within a tolerance and we have to control the finished weight within a tolerance. This is the operation that allows that to happen.

When the projectiles have left the heat-treating furnace, you can tell they've been heat-treated by the darkness of color. They have some scale on the outside, but that doesn't bother us, because we're going to finish the projectile on the outside at a later time. But the inside of the projectile is very important because nothing else is going to be done to the projectile until we finish painting the inside of it. Then, of course, it gets filled with explosives. So this operation takes a projectile, loads it onto its nose, and with forced air takes steel shot and shot-blasts the inside of the projectile to clean it up. The operator then inspects the inside because it is very important that we don't have any flaws, any crevices, or anything in the projectiles that would hamper the loading or the performance of the projectile. (11)

Next comes the final operation for the 120-millimeter projectile. The projectile has been fiber-coated, and it's been phosphate-lubed all over. We do some hand-painting to the holes and the notches in it. The conveyor takes the projectile to the finish-coat stage, where we control wet film thickness, dry film thickness, and adhesion. Then the projectile, after curing for 24 hours, is subjected to a 72-hour salt spray, in which it must withstand a salt impregnation without rusting. The projectile then goes through a drying tunnel, where it is air-dried, and is then loaded into boxes and readied for shipment. Each paint lot has to pass salt-spray inspection, because when firing through a mortar tube, the paint thickness of the projectile becomes very important. (12)

The United States government determines the color of the projectile. The white color is a designation for a smoke projectile. If the projectile were painted blue, it would be designated as a training projectile, and if it were painted olive drab or green, that would be the designation of a high-explosive loaded projectile. ⑬

The paint booth is expertly controlled, in that we control the air going through the booth. We move so many cubic feet of air per minute over a filtering system that filters the paint and exhaust to the outside of the building. Due to Pennsylvania environmental laws, this paint is called a volatile organic compound.

At the back side of the paint booth the finished projectiles go through their final inspection. One of the most critical things about the final inspection is that we ring-gauge the projectile to make sure the diameter on the outside is exactly the right size. The worst thing that could happen would be if the diameter were oversized and the projectile lodged in the tube during firing.

Chamberlain manufactured 75-millimeter projectiles for French artillery pieces used on the Western Front in World War I.

After final inspection we lube the threads on both the front and the back, put on protective caps, put a sleeve on it to protect the paint, and load it into a cardboard box. The projectile is then held until we pass salt-spray inspection. After the salt-spray inspection, the shells are shipped out to the load plant, where they're loaded with either the explosive or the gas that they hold. ⑭

Cove

1 • 8 • 8 • 3

Location	Cove Shoes 107 Highland Street Martinsburg, PA 16662 (814) 793-3786 www.coveshoe.com
Hours	No public tours available. Factory outlet store on premises.
Tour Guide	Bob LaRochelle Superintendent of Manufacturing

What we're going to show you today is the largest heavy-duty footwear manu-facturing facility in North America. We do private-label footwear for companies like Ralph Lauren/Polo, L.L. Bean, Harley-Davidson, Fry Boots, Cabella's, and Bass Pro Shops. We also do a wide range of military footwear. In addition to that, about

1

30 to 40 percent of what we make has a steel toe in it. So we do a lot of workplace and safety-type footwear. ①

Right now we're in the warehouse where all of our raw materials come in. This is where we store all of the leathers, heels, soles, nails, eyelets, hooks—all of the different parts that go into making the shoe. In this warehouse we have at all times at least a million feet of upper leathers of all different colors for the different companies we manufacture for.

What you are looking at is a hide that has had different parts of the shoe stapled on it. ② The purpose of that is to show new cutters where to take different parts of the shoe from to

maximize the hide. If parts of the shoes are not taken from a proper location, the shoes will not hold their shape properly. That's the reason for this picture.

People usually don't realize the difficulty involved in cutting the leather for these shoes. All of our shoes are cut in 12-pair lots. That means the cutter has got to concentrate on keeping track of the number of individual parts, because it takes 24 vamps for 12 pairs. It takes 48 quarters for 12 pairs. It takes 24 back straps, 24 counter pockets, 24 gussets. These are all different parts of the shoes that he must keep track of as he cuts so he doesn't cut more parts than are needed for that particular size shoe. Cutters have to be very selective when they cut, so they don't include the leather brand marks in the shoes, or tick marks, or scars, or anything that will make a shoe look like it's defective. ③

The cutter you see on the following page is cutting an inside counter pocket that will be on the inside of the shoe. She uses different dies to make sure she uses as much as possible of the roll of leather. Leather generally runs between $2.50 and $3.00 a foot, and we want to throw away as little as possible so we can keep our costs in line and make our shoes competitive. She's now cutting the front part that goes over the toes. That's called the vamp. In the process of cutting, she's looking for defects in the leather, and she's cutting the leather directionally so that the shoe will hold its shape properly. ④

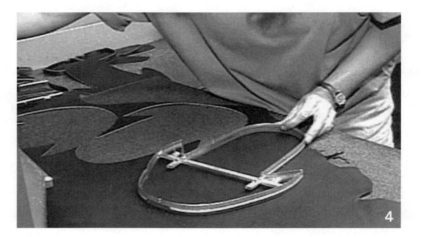

It's hard to visualize a shoe right now, but as we go on through the process you'll see that it's going to come together.

This is where we brand different logos for different manufacturers on parts of the shoes. This is done in a heat process with pressure. It's almost like what the cowboys used to do when they branded a cow, except that we don't use as much heat. And since we don't have a cow, we don't have to tie the cow up. This happens to be the Red Head brand, and is being made for Bass Pro. ⑤

> Cove Shoes has been located at its 200,000-square-foot facility in Martinsburg, PA, for more than 40 years, and today employs 450 people.

> The United States Marine Corps is now using Matterhorn boots, made by Cove Shoes. They are lighter, cooler, more shock-absorbent, and more water-resistant than the traditional combat boot. Cowhide has been replaced with GORE-TEX and Teflon.

There are different stitching operations where different parts of the shoes are being assembled. Here we see the tongue being put onto the vamp. ⑥ This happens to be a Harley-Davidson boot. We make many different styles of Harley boots. We are one of their top manufacturers.

As you can see, all of these operations are done by hand. Even though we have sewing machines that are automatic, there is no preset automated system that makes

any particular part of the shoe. Each operator must control it himself. That's why the shoe industry is considered a craft industry. Because everything is done by hand, you really have to be a craftsman to make shoes.

What we are stitching here is a webbing. ⑦ The webbing is used in Corcoran jump boots. It's been a tradition with military people, especially paratroopers, to have these boots with the webbing as a support for the ankles when landing. Being a former paratrooper myself, I assure you that was the only boot that I used to wear. I take

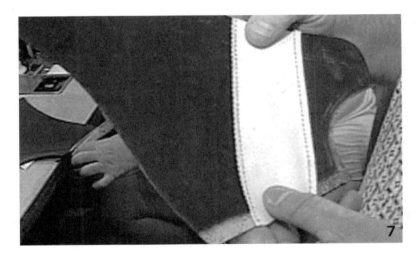

particular pride in making sure that our Corcoran boots are made better than any jump boot you can buy. Not only am I a past paratrooper, but I also have a son who's currently a paratrooper. He's in the 82nd Airborne Division. So I want to make sure that if he buys a pair of our boots, they are made perfectly.

Most of our footwear is made with an American flag on it. You don't find that very often anymore, since about 90 percent of the footwear sold in the United States is imported. So when you see the flag on a shoe, it may very well have been made in Martinsburg, PA.

We're about to enter the main fitting room. There are approximately 95 people who work in this department, assembling all the different parts that it takes to make a shoe.

It's now beginning to look like a boot. It has the back, the counter pocket, and the webbing that supports the ankles for paratrooper boots. And that's what this happens to be. This is an HH-brand jump boot. ⑧

The next operation is called flaming and trimming. This is where we trim all of the loose threads off the shoes so that when you pick up a shoe it looks neat and clean, without thread ends hanging all over it. We have to be very careful in this process because a lot of these shoes may have synthetic leather linings in them, and if you hit that with a flame, you burn it right off. So great care has to be taken in flaming and trimming these thread ends off the shoes. ⑨

The assembly area is where we match the uppers of the shoes to the outer soles and the inner soles. This is the "last" that the shoe is made on. ⑩ If you look at it, you can see it looks like a foot. We have these in all different sizes and widths. This happens to be a 12D. We have a last for each size in Ds, Es, EEs, and EEEs; we have some in As and Bs, depending on the particular style of shoe that we're making.

When the shoe goes through this area, we attach the insole, which is the foundation of the shoe. The insoles come in varying shapes and materials. This is called the pillow insole. ⑪ It is a half-inch cushion that's wrapped with a Dry-lex lining. The Dry-lex lining is constructed so that it will absorb moisture from the foot and pull it down to the bottom of the shoe so that the foot always stays dry. And you can see, from the thickness of the foam, that comfort is also involved.

Here a steel toe is being put onto our safety toe shoes. ⑫ A hot-melt machine is used so that when the steel toe is put on, it will stay in place. A piece of felt is inserted to ensure comfort so that the steel does not bite into the foot after the manufacturing process is complete.

This shoe also has a piece of KEVLAR to try to make the toe chainsaw-resistant. So if you happen to be working in the lumber industry and you are using a chainsaw and it comes down and hits your shoe, this may not stop it, but it will minimize the injury to your foot.

In the making room, Joe is trimming the excess leather around the shoe. If we don't do that, the leather gets in the way when we start sewing. Joe makes a very difficult job look very simple. ⑬

After this step we are able to remove the tacks from the sole. Insole tacks are used in the shoes to hold the inner sole

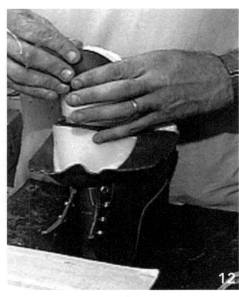

in place while the shoe is going through the lasting and the making room. Every tack has to be removed from the shoe or they can cause injury to the foot. To give you some idea of the concentration that is needed on a job that a lot of people may consider to be simple, this week we will pack 18,600 pairs of shoes. That's 37,200 shoes. With five tacks per shoe, it comes out to 186,000 tacks that must be removed.

Our people realize the importance of removing tacks and they do an absolutely terrific job making sure they are all removed. We have four different inspection systems throughout the factory that check for tacks that were left on the inside, and if we find five tacks a day it's amazing. And you can only do this if you have people who are truly dedicated to what they do.

This is what's known as the soling area, where we attach the soles to the bottom of the shoes. ⑭ The sole is heat-activated; it is put on the bottom of the shoe and put into the press. The press squeezes it together, and it is ready to have the sole stitched on.

The finishing room is where we finish the bottoms of the shoes. Here we are about to start heeling some Western boots. The base and the lip are assembled onto the boot and nailed on with wire nails. We make sure that when the boot is put in, it is aligned. Again, it looks very simple but if that shoe isn't held exactly right, the heel will be crooked. ⑮

At this point all of the major operations have been completed and we're going to do the finishing work. Here we're taking a shoe that has a kind of raw-edge sole on it and we're staining it to make it look one color. This is all done by hand, since there is no other way to do it. You'd have to be very careful not to get that edge stain on the upper because chances are it won't come off. ⑯

Founded in 1883, Cove Shoe Company is now a division of H.H. Brown Shoe Company, a wholly owned subsidiary of Berkshire Hathaway, Inc.

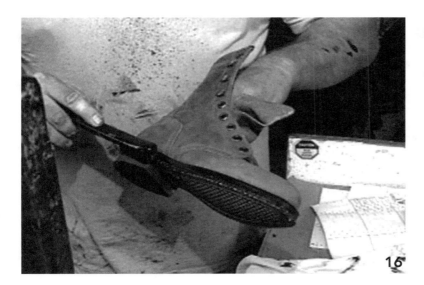

The final step is where the shoes are inspected. This is a finished Matterhorn GORE-TEX boot. This boot is sold to people in the service, just like the Corcoran jump boot is. It is a waterproof Thinsulate boot. It's the boot that was worn in Bosnia when our troops first went over there. We shipped 40,000 pairs over very quickly because it was in wintertime, and this is the boot that kept their feet warm and dry. And we received hundreds and hundreds of letters from the servicepeople thanking us for designing and building this shoe. ⑰

FROGSWITCH

Location	Frog, Switch and Manufacturing
	600 East High Street
	Carlisle, PA 17013
	(717) 243-2454
	www.frogswitch.com
Hours	Public tours available by appointment only.
Tour Guide	Karl Funk
	Process Engineer

Hello, and welcome to the Frog, Switch and Manufacturing Company in Carlisle, PA. We are manufacturers of manganese steel castings, primarily used in the crushing and grinding industry. Manganese steel is a steel that's very well known for its toughness and resistance to wear. The company has a long history. It was founded in 1881 by Mr. John Hayes, and to this day continues to be family owned and operated. The company got its start in the manufacturing of railcars. It eventually evolved into railroad track work, and then crushing and grinding parts. A question often asked about the name of the company, Frog, Switch and Manufacturing, is, "What exactly does the name mean?" Anybody who has seen railroad tracks knows

that there are switches, and the switches have two main components: the actual switch points, which direct the trains onto different tracks; and the frog, which is where the outer rail crosses the inner rail. Frogs made up a very big part of this company's business over the years. (1)

During the 1960s, the company made the decision to get out of the railroad business and continue on with crushing and grinding equipment. Since the name Frog, Switch was very well known in the industry for manganese steel, it was natural to keep the name as we continued into the 1970s, 1980s, and 1990s in the rock-crushing business.

We're going to start our tour in the pattern shop. The art of metal castings goes back over 3,000 years, and was originated by the Chinese. And three things have not changed since that time. In order to make a steel casting you need molten metal, a mold in which to pour the metal to get the shape you want, and a pattern to make that shape. Here in the pattern shop is where we make that pattern. We have six highly skilled craftsmen who are involved in making the wood pattern from which the castings are made. ②

Since we've been in business over 100 years, we have over 20,000 patterns on hand, about 3,000 to 5,000 of which are active at any given time. A pattern mill specializes in making round parts, which are the bulk of the type we make. We have a fairly well-equipped pattern shop with all different types of woodworking equipment. We have table saws, joiners, planers, and, of course, the mill.

The foundry is where we produce the molds that will be used to hold the molten metal to get our final shapes. We use two different methods of molding here at Frog, Switch. One is called the V process, or vacuum process, and the other is called the no-bake process. What you're looking at here is a V process mold. ③

There are two halves of the machine: the top half, which is called the cope, and the bottom half, which is the drag. The idea here is to take a film of plastic and drape it across the pattern. The next step will be to fill it with sand, at which time another sheet of plastic will be draped across. Air is sucked out of the sand, creating a very rigid mold. There is nothing holding this sand together except for the vacuum. It's almost rock-hard, yet if you reach under the plastic and grab a handful of sand, it's very, very loose. An analogy that sometimes helps people understand is their vacuum-packed coffee. If you have ever had one of those vacuum-packed pouches of coffee, you know how hard they are, and when you open it up, you have loose coffee. That's exactly the same principle we have here.

Here you can see the plastic being draped over the pattern, and you can see the vacuum pulling that plastic tight. (4) The vacuum process has several advantages

over conventional casting processes. One is the rate of replication. The pattern always stays put, so we are able to turn out molds from this same pattern time after time after time. And because this plastic is between the sand and the pattern, there is very little pattern wear. So the pattern does not wear out over time as in conventional pattern-casting processes.

This process, the V process, was developed by the Japanese in the 1970s. The first unit was installed here at Frog, Switch in the late 1970s, and we've had two units installed since then. This has actually been responsible for a turnaround at Frog, Switch. This process has helped us maintain our competitive edge in the marketplace and helped us capture a large portion of business that we otherwise would have lost if we had not switched to the V process.

Here we have half of a mold that's been completed. (5) Now we will strip the top half, or the cope, off the molding machine, bring it here and set it down, close this mold up, and make it complete and ready for pouring.

Here the top half of the mold is being lifted off of the pattern. ⑥ Again, that shows you the advantage of the V process: the pattern stays in place. Next we'll poke some holes in the plastic to allow for some venting once the molten metal is poured in there. It will aid in drafting off some of the casting's gases, which could cause defects in the casting.

All the molds we have on line are hooked up to vacuum lines. We've got over 1,000 horsepower of vacuum running at this plant to keep these molds on line. If we would lose power for whatever reason—a lightning storm, an accident that takes a pole down—and the vacuum system goes down, every mold that's on line is lost because the vacuum must be maintained at all times.

Next we will apply what's called a mold wash, which is a material that protects the surface of the mold. It acts as a barrier between the sand and the molten metal. It also helps to keep the mold together as the molten metal is filling the mold. If there's any overspill or dribbling of molten metal we want to avoid burning through the plastic, because if we burn through the plastic, we lose vacuum. If we lose vacuum, the whole mold will fall right out. ⑦

A long-term plant modernization program, started in the early 1970s, is still in place and has resulted in a 100 percent increase in plant capacity.

This is our V-3 molding station. (8) It's very similar to what you saw earlier, but we believe they are the largest production vacuum-processed castings made in the world. Castings weight on V-3 can go up to 13,000 pounds, with a typical weight being 5,000 to 6,000 pounds. Here again the plastic is drawn on the pattern, and what we're doing is assembling the appendages, the risers, and the gating system that will be used to complete the casting. The process is essentially identical to the smaller-scale molding line but on a much larger scale. Instead of having several thousand pounds contained with that sheet of plastic that is five thousandths of an inch thick, here you're talking about 15 tons of sand that will be held with the vacuum.

We're now getting ready to place the V-3 flask on the pattern carrier. When the flask is in place, we fill the mold with sand. As the sand starts filling the mold, the table it sits on will start to vibrate. This helps to compress the sand, so it fills the mold very compactly. (9)

When the mold is filled, we strike off the sand and make it even all the way across. Then we hook up the vacuum to start drawing the air out of the sand. Now we'll spread a sheet of plastic, which will seal the vacuum. Then we'll tape up the ends of the plastic from top to bottom so it doesn't snag and come loose.

The mold is then ready to strip off the pattern carrier. What we're going to do now is lift the pattern completely off the carrier and roll it over. Now keep in mind there's about seven tons of sand in there being held together by thin sheets of plastic. What we'll do next is take the mold down to the shop and put it in place for pouring. Once the drag of the casting is in place, the second half, which is the cope, will come down, and then we'll close the mold and it will be ready for pouring. ⑩

When the molding process is completed, it's time to prepare our batch of steel. We have a couple of different varieties of scrap that we use to make up a heat of manganese steel. We purchase manganese steel scrap and scrap castings plus foundry returns that we keep in one area of our plant. Keep in mind that manganese steel is nonmagnetic, so we cannot use a magnet to lift this material around; we must use a mechanical grabber. The other part of our batch is plain old plate steel scrap, which is recycled from various fabricators of plate steel. The arc operator gets a computer printout from the office that tells him exactly what percentage of each type of material has to go into that charge to get the desired chemistry. ⑪

This is one of our two furnaces. (12) They are 10-ton, direct-arc furnaces. We have three electrodes on the top, which put about 14,000 amps' worth of electricity into that furnace. We're able to melt 22,000 pounds of steel in about an hour and a half to two hours. This furnace has been running for about two hours now, and the metal is all molten. Next the operator takes his preliminary sample. This is a small sample of metal where we check our chemistry to make sure we're on target. And whatever we need to add to the furnace we calculate by computer. So right now what he's doing is his preliminary sample. That sample will be cooled with water, and we'll take it down to the lab and check the chemistry. If the chemistry is right, we'll go ahead and tap the heat.

Company founder John Zug was a businessman, editor, publisher, attorney, and entrepreneur. In 1898, he reorganized the Carlisle Manufacturing Company into the Frog, Switch and Manufacturing Company, which went on to become a leader in the manufacture of steel parts for railroads.

12

When the sample comes down from the furnace, we have to prepare it for analysis. For that we have a service grinder here, which cuts below the surface of the metal so we get down to good, clean metal. We'll cool the sample off in the water, and then sand it to a 60-grit finish. You need to have a 60-grit finish to get a good analysis on the spectrographic unit. That unit is an instrument where the sample is burned with a high-voltage spark. The light from that burning sample is collected by the instrument, where it's divided into its different wavelengths. Each element in the sample gives off a different wavelength, and there are sensors that measure the intensity of each of those wavelengths. Then it is turned into a numerical percentage for carbon, manganese, silicon, chrome, nickel, etc. We are aiming for a certain grade of material up in the furnace. So when we find out what we have, the computer will automatically compare it against what we're trying to get and calculate what raw materials need to be added to bring the steel to specifications. Those results will be fed up to the melt deck by computer, and the melt furnace operator will know exactly what material to put into the furnace before we get back up there. (13)

Now we're ready to tap the heat. The furnace is on a mechanical tilt mechanism, and the operator will roll the furnace forward to get the metal to tap out. The tapping temperature of the steel is approximately 2,750 degrees Fahrenheit, and we'll pour our castings at about 2,630 degrees. The pouring spout on our furnace is spe-

cially designed so as the metal taps out, it automatically separates the slag, which is the waste material that floats to the top. As the furnace starts to tilt further, the slag will start to tap off and spill into the collection pit. You can see the slag starting to be tapped off the right side and collecting in the pit. After the tapping of the furnace is complete, the operator must take his final sample for analysis and also check the temperature. The temperature is recorded, and the ladle then goes to the ladle station to prepare for pouring the castings. (14)

Founded in 1881 and in the same location for 120 years, the company has 200 employees who work in a plant that occupies 175,000 square feet of space.

Now we're ready to pour the castings. The crane will pick the ladle up and place it on top of the mold. The metal comes out through the bottom of the ladle into the pouring cup, which then goes in the mold. The ladle man also has a scale on the hook of the crane to determine how much metal he has to ladle at all times. He has to line up his pour spout over the pour cup of the mold, so he's assured the metal will go into the mold with minimum spillage. The nozzle is now open and the metal is filling the molds. It takes about 40 seconds to fill a mold, and it takes about 8,000 pounds of metal. (15)

When the casting cools and is removed from the sand, you can see that it still has some appendages on it. These appendages must be removed before we can process the casting further. The interesting thing about manganese steel is that even though it's famous for its toughness, when it's taken out of the mold in the green condition, as we call it, it is extremely brittle. In fact, if you take one of these large castings in this condition and drop it, chances are it will break in half. To develop the toughness of the manganese steel, we must reheat it. Here in the heat-treat facility we have four furnaces. We take that manganese steel casting, heat it to 2,000 degrees Fahrenheit, hold it for between four and eight hours, then quench it rapidly in water to bring it back down to room temperature. This is the process that gives manganese steel its legendary toughness for crushing and grinding applications. (16)

Once the castings come out of heat-treat, they are ready for final finishing. This machine here is a good example of how we have brought tooling of manganese steel to the highest end of technology. This is our newest addition to the company, a very large vertical boring mill with a 12-foot table. It's actually a 1953 Giddings and Lewis machine that was updated last year with the most modern technology. This machine is a work horse for our company, and we're very proud to have it here. We have a carbide insert cutting the manganese steel, which, as we talked about before, is very tough and a very difficult material to machine. This particular part is called a mantle. It's used for crushing of iron ore and copper ore in the very large mines. The part being machined here is the mounting surface, which will be mounted onto the crushing machine. (17)

Once the castings are machined, they go to the inspection area. We measure to make sure the dimensions of the cast are right and also do a visual inspection to make sure there are no defects, such as holes, or gas pockets, or any protrusions on the surface. The castings may have a number of destinations once they're inspected and painted. Some may go directly to the end user in a quarry or a mine; some may go to an original equipment manufacturer such as a crusher manufacturer. It does vary, but we make sure the castings are ready, wherever they're going.

HERR'S

Location	Herr's Foods
	Routes 1 and 272
	Nottingham, PA 19362
	(800) 63-SNACK
	www.herrs.com
Hours	Public tours available Monday through Thursday, 9:00 a.m. to 3:00 p.m.; Friday, 9:00 a.m. to 11:00 a.m. Gift and memorabilia shop on premises.
Tour Guide	Phil Bernas
	Manufacturing Technical Manager

The first thing that we need to make pretzels is raw ingredients, and the main raw ingredient is flour. This is very much like the flour you have in your own home. What we are using is soft-bread winter wheat flour, which is much like the flour you use at home in making bread, cookies, and cakes. This flour is made especially for Herr's. It is planted in the fall, it is dormant in the wintertime, and it is harvested in the spring. This flour is grown in Pennsylvania, Illinois, Indiana, and Ohio, and we get it delivered to our plant about twice daily in 50,000-pound trailers. This is the lifeblood of all pretzels. (1)

Another ingredient that we use is bicarbonates, which are used to leaven the product. They are chemical leavening agents, which actually raise the product to give it a little bit of body and texture. One of the other chief ingredients that we use is yeast, which is a natural leavener. This does the same thing as chemical leaveners, but gives the pretzels a particular flavor that we're looking for.

Another chief ingredient is malt, which we use in the form of malted corn syrup, much like the corn syrup you might use in your own home. A malt is really the chief flavor ingredient in most pretzels.

1

What we're going to do now is add those ingredients and mix our dough. ② We add a little bit of yeast, and our malted corn syrup for flavor, and then mix a 300-pound bag of flour with two double-arm mixers. It actually kneads the dough and pulls the dough together. Everything is in our pretzel mix right now except water, and that will be added once the mixer door is closed. The pretzel dough will mix for six minutes at about 28 RPMs [revolutions per minute], and that mixing action is pulling the dough together, and combining the protein in the flour with the water to form a thing we call gluten.

Our finished product is a dough mixture much like this. ③ As you can see, the gluten, which is the Latin word for glue, is actually causing the dough to stick together. So there is a certain stretch, a certain elasticity, within our dough that we are looking for to make pretzels.

When the dough is finished mixing it is dropped down into a dough box. This is a continuous-extrusion system that forces the dough out through a small opening, and it is formed into small loaves. The small loaves are delivered to our mixer systems, or our extrusion systems.

In the Herr's oven room, the dough that is dropped from the mixer systems goes into a shuttle system that delivers the dough into five separate compartments. These compartments have their own auger system, which pushes the dough through individual die plates. The die plates vary on the pretzel. On the following page you see a die plate that makes the traditional pretzel shape. ④ On the back side of the die plate are metering holes, which the dough is pushed through. The dough pushes through from this side, is formed into the pretzel shape on the other side, and is knitted together to form the pretzel that we know.

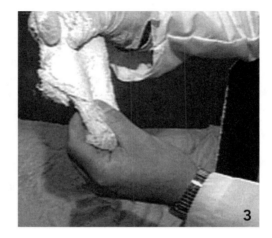

Pretzels can be made into almost any shape imaginable. This particular pretzel is not a traditional pretzel shape, but more of a rod shape. ⑤ This is the type of die opening that we have in this pretzel extruder. The other side of it is a series of metering holes where the dough is pushed through. It finally meets on the other side to form the pretzel rod.

The next area is where the pretzel dough is cut into shapes. We use what we call a guillotine knife cutting system, actually one long series of blades cutting the pretzel dough into small, one-inch pieces. The pretzels have a long ride to take, actually a 20-minute ride on a proofing table, before they go into a pretzel oven. The long ride on the proofing table allows the pretzels to develop texture, volume, and flavor. The combination of the yeast action, working with the bulk, can cause a fermentation process, producing the flavors that are desirable in a sourdough product. ⑥

After a ride on the proofing belt for 20 to 25 minutes, the pretzels are covered with a sodium solution, which gelatinizes the starches, or makes the starch in the pretzel dough sticky. It also provides an adhering surface for the pretzel salt. The

sodium solution provides the browning color in the baking process that gives finished pretzels their familiar look.

After the pretzels are covered with the sodium solution, they are very sticky and gelatinized. So it provides a very good adherent surface for salt. When the salt is applied to the surface, it adheres very well. About 50 percent of the salt that's applied to the pretzels adheres to it, and the other 50 percent is returned and recycled. This all happens before the baking process. ⑦

Once the pretzels enter the baking chamber, they go through a very long tunnel oven, about 100 feet long. Inside that oven are a series of 17 to 20 burners going above and below the product. The pretzels travel along on a moving screen through the oven. The whole baking process takes approximately 12 minutes.

Most of the baking takes place in the center of the oven, and most of the browning occurs near the end of the oven. The atmosphere of the oven is also very tightly controlled, and it has a series of exhaust fans, which exhaust the moisture that's driven off the pretzels during the baking. Creating perfect moisture conditions inside the oven is very critical in baking pretzels. After 12 minutes inside the oven, you can see the result: a nice toasty-brown color with salt adhering to the surface. The pretzel right now is fully baked but is not completely dried. In other words, it is not in its finished form. The pretzels at this stage have about 13 percent moisture. ⑧

> The company's full line of snacks consists of more than 280 items, including potato chips, pretzels, tortilla chips, cheese curls, popcorn, crackers, nuts, pork rinds, onion rings, and meat sticks.

The pretzels then drop down into another stage that is a much slower process, and that is being dried in a drying kiln. The pretzel temperatures inside the baking oven sometimes reach as high as 700 degrees Fahrenheit, but when the pretzels drop into the lower stage, they are dried for long periods of time, sometimes as much as 90 minutes, at lower temperatures, 250 to 270 degrees Fahrenheit. There they are brought down to a finished moisture of about 3 to 4 percent. It's at this point that the pretzel is done. The entire process from beginning to end will take somewhere in the neighborhood of 2 to $2\frac{1}{2}$ hours—from mixing, to extrusion, to proofing, to baking, to drying—before the finished pretzel is packaged. ⑨

The entire process is computer-controlled. This keeps the oven temperatures exactly the same throughout the day, it keeps the pressure inside the oven exactly the same through the day, and keeps the moisture level inside the oven exactly the same. All the formulas are stored inside the computer, so when a product is ready to start, it remembers all of the last details of the process. The computerized controls on the pretzel ovens and the extrusion process virtually eliminate any variability in our product.

This is the traditional pretzel that most people are familiar with, after the pretzel dough is extruded through the die plates that we showed you earlier.⑩ Here a high-speed band cuts the pretzels into quality-controlled pretzel weights that can be baked evenly in our ovens. This particular extruder is running at about 120 strokes per minute, and is making approximately one million pretzels every two hours. That is a lot faster than making them by hand.

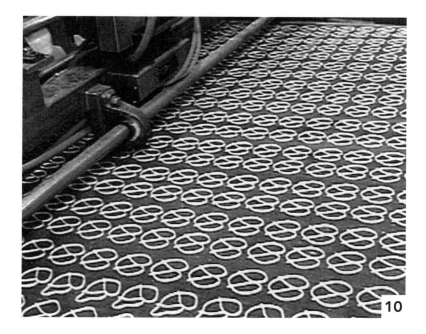
10

These traditional pretzels, instead of being run under a waterfall of sodium solution, are run into a bath of sodium solution and are completely submerged, usually for a period of 10 to 13 seconds. They become gelatinized and sticky so salt will adhere to them. This process is much shorter. The actual baking process is only about three minutes. The drying process is only about 20 minutes. The entire process of making this pretzel is usually only 30 minutes.

After being baked at about 600 degrees Fahrenheit for three minutes, the pretzels contain a moisture content of 10 to 13 percent. This is the intermediate stage. After they are baked for three minutes, they are dropped down into a drying kiln, and after about 20 minutes at 270 degrees, they are dried to a finished product moisture of about 2 percent.

In the Herr's packing room, the pretzels that have moved out of the oven are allowed to cool down a little bit and are now distributed to a weigh head. These weigh heads are calibrated to calculate the amount of product for the size of bag we want. There are 14 individual scales. These scales will weigh out the products, and then precisely dump the exact weight into the bag that the net weight calls for. ⑪

After the pretzels are weighed, they are dropped down a transition chute into a form-and-fill bag. The packaging film is usually polypropylene, which keeps moisture and air out, and keeps the product fresh. Some packaging machines can run up to 120 bags a minute. Once the bag is formed, it goes through a seal check area that checks for any leaks in the bag, making sure the consumer does not get a bag with a hole in it. Then the product is transferred to our automatic case packers. These automatically count the bags in a case and deliver the case to the warehouse. After the case is filled, it is automatically closed, identified with a label, and then sent to the warehouse.

JUST BORN®

·

QUALITY CONFECTIONS

Location	Just Born
	1300 Stefko Boulevard
	Bethlehem, PA 18016
	(610) 867-7568
	www.justborn.com
Hours	Public tours not available.
Tour Guide	Frank Olszewski
	Packaging Engineer

Welcome to Just Born Candies in Bethlehem, PA. A lot of folks ask us how we got our name. Born is the family name of our founding father, Sam Born, who started the company as part of a confectionery business in New York City. He and his cousins moved the operation here to Bethlehem in 1932. A lot of people recognize us more for our products, Mike and Ike jelly beans and marshmallow Peeps, than by our company name. ①

Here in our Bethlehem plant we make more than 20 billion jelly beans a year, and we are processing more marshmallow candies than any other company in the country. If you would like to put on your hair net and follow me, we'll show you how we make jelly beans and marshmallow Peeps.

We're going to start our tour in our mogul cooking area. We have two moguls

here in the Just Born plant. In this area we produce the cooked slurry, which is a sweet liquid we use to make our jelly bean centers. This system is completely automated. All of our ingredients are weighed out automatically and passed through the various steam kettles to be cooked into a liquid form, and then they're passed through the piping system into the molds.

We use molds made of starch for forming jelly bean centers. As the molds move down the line they go into our liquid-filling area, and liquid slurry is injected into the impressions in the starch molds. The molds containing the centers are then stacked and taken to our curing ovens.

Here we take the raw jelly bean centers and put them in a large tumbling device we call a pan. In the pan we alternate layers of sugar, flavoring, and color. We take the candy out of the pan when the jelly beans achieve the weight that we desire. Our panning crew works a very early shift. They come in usually at 4 or 5 o'clock in the morning and finish up early in the afternoon. ②

In Building 4 we have one of our two packaging areas. All of our packaging machinery is fed in essentially the same manner. We dump our candy through a screen to remove candy that might have stuck together during the panning operation—lumps of candy, if you will. In this bin we are making what we refer to as our original Mike and Ike mix. We have lime, orange, cherry, and lemon flavors. We first screen the candy, then we mix the candy manually as it moves up the bed of the bin. The candy will then feed into a bucket elevator and go up to our scale unit, where it is weighed for packaging. ③

Now we're up on top of the scale unit. This particular scale unit is weighing out candy for five-pound bags. ④ We have a series of small hoppers in a merry-go-round arrangement, and they will give us the required amount of candy that we need

down below in the packaging machine. We make more than 20 billion jelly beans a year. That's enough jelly beans to go around the world more than four times. ⑤

> The factory has been in the same location since 1931. The company currently occupies 500,000 square feet of space, and employs 400 people.

> Yellow Peeps are the most popular, followed by pink, lavender, blue, and white.

> In 1953, it took 27 hours to create one marshmallow Peep. Today, it takes six minutes.

Here in the plant we use more than 24 million pounds of sugar a year and over 20 million pounds of corn syrup. If you consider the standard paper sugar packets you might get in a restaurant, we use enough sugar in a year that, if laid end-to-end, those packets would circle the world twice.

On the following page you see our five-pound-bag packaging machine. ⑥ We're dropping the candy from the scales that we just saw. The film we use to form the bags comes in a flat roll and is passed through these rollers. That flat film passes over a forming tube and goes down along the tube, where it is heat-sealed. As the bags are formed, they drop onto a conveyor, and what we have is a brand-new five-pound bag of Mike and Ike candy. The candy then passes through a metal

detector and up to our packaging area. We pack everything from a four-ounce bag to a five-pound bag. ⑦

We currently have 10 packaging lines here in the plant. Typically, we will operate five or six of those on any given shift. We operate three shifts a day, five days a week, and we normally operate at least one shift on Saturday.

In our pilot plant area we make test runs of candy. We test new flavors and new combinations of flavors, try different ingredients, maybe try out new suppliers, and test the results. It gives us an idea of what we might encounter if we go full scale in the plant. What we do is use centers right from the plant, bring them in here, and build up the candy and polish it. Today we are working on our orange flavor to make sure the flavor is there and the color is correct. We also have a small unit here where we can process limited quantities of marshmallow and run test batches. ⑧

We've come to our marshmallow cooking area. We're in front of what's referred to as our "Bob" kettle. ⑨ "Bob" is an industry term. Here we batch our initial corn syrup and granulated and liquid sugars, and we put that mix in this steam-jacketed kettle to boil off the excess water. The kettle itself is controlled and automated so that we control our ingredients. We heat the liquid mixture to roughly 240 degrees and boil off the excess water until we have a mixture that gives us the proper solid content. At that point we take that liquid slurry, as we call it, and pump it over to one of our large blending kettles. Then we add additional corn syrup and gelatin, to give the marshmallow some body, and a little bit of vanilla flavoring. As this mixture is blended, we pass it over to one of our four cooling kettles.

In addition to making marshmallow Peeps and bunnies for Easter, Just Born also makes marshmallow cats, pumpkins, and ghosts for Halloween, and marshmallow trees and snowmen for Christmas.

The original marshmallow Peeps were squeezed one at a time out of a pastry tube, and the eyes were painted on by hand. Today the company can add 3,500 Peeps' eyes per minute.

In the cooling kettles we continue to blend. ⑩ As the slurry exits these kettles, it passes through one of our two Oakes machines. "Oakes" is the name of the manufacturer of the equipment. What we do in that machine is the same thing you do at home when you are beating egg whites. We inject air into the slurry mixture, and it gives it a nice white, fluffy texture. From that Oakes machine we pipe the slurry across to one of what we call the depositing belts. We prepare the belts by adding

colored sugar, which we prepared ahead of time by spraying white granulated sugar. We add that to the belt through a screen system, which deposits a nice uniform layer on the belt. And then, as the marshmallow comes through the piping system and through the depositor, it drops onto that bed of colored sugar.

The marshmallow passes through a pair of counter-revolving rollers and is pushed through a die. That die gives the marshmallow its shape. The marshmallow goes through the die; in this case it is a bunny die. ⑪ The marshmallow passes through and then is sheared off by a mechanical arm. In order to put color on the entire piece, we pass it through an air chamber where we blow the sugar down onto it. The sugar then adheres to the moist, warm marshmallow. As it exits the chamber—you could refer to it as a sugar shower—it comes out completely coated.

Here is what we refer to as our Number One belt, or "Peep belt." ⑫ As you see our Peeps "walking" up the belt here, they are going into the air chamber where

they are subjected to the same sugar shower that the bunnies were. As the candy comes up the belt, we remove the excess sugar from the surface by passing it under a manifold system where we blow air across it and blow off that excess sugar.

As the candy comes up the belt there are no decorations on it. As it passes under the decorating head, which is optically controlled, we spray the decorations on the candy. So the bunnies essentially come in here blind, and they leave with eyes. We have controls at the upstream end that tell us if the candy is slightly off line. If so, the entire carriage will move to compensate so that the eyes are placed properly on the candy. ⑬

We've been asked why the Peeps come up the belt backwards. We like to tell people that they are so anxious to get into the cartons, and onto the grocery shelves for people to buy, that we don't want them to see where they are going. That way

13

they don't get too excited and at least they stay in position long enough for us to put the eyes on. ⑭

14

The candy then passes into an elevator. The elevator raises the trays under a precut piece of cellophane, which is folded over the top and heat-sealed. The trays then pass down the line after sealing, through the metal detector, and into the packaging area where we place each in cartons.

Most of our bunnies are packaged in combinations. Here we're packaging three clusters in a single tray. On another part of the belt we are packing four clusters in a tray. ⑮

As the candy goes through the over-wrap machine, it passes through the metal detector. This is a system we use throughout the plant, and it is used throughout the food industry to make sure that you and I as consumers don't end up with something in the food that we're not supposed to get. The likelihood of that happening is not very great, but in any operation there is always the remote possibility. That's why the metal detectors are placed at the end of the line. The last thing we do before material leaves the plant is assure ourselves that the product is safe.

15

Location	KME Fire Apparatus
	One Industrial Complex
	Nesquehoning, PA 18240
	(800) 235-3928
	www.kovatch.com
Hours	Public tours not available.
Tour Guide	John J. Kovatch III
	President

Hello and welcome to KME Fire Apparatus, a leading manufacturer of custom-built fire trucks. We're in our chassis assembly plant in the frame buildup area. This is the first step in the manufacturing of a custom chassis. All of the frame rails are laid out on AutoCAD. All of the hole locations are placed, and holes are then pierced into the frame to ensure the utmost squareness of the frame. After comple-

tion of the piercing process, the frame rails are trimmed to length and we begin the assembly. The assembly of the frame rail consists of the frame assembly, the suspension, the steering gear, pump mounts, and cross members. ①

While the chassis frame is being plumbed, the engine assembly is being prepared for the chassis. In this area the engines are equipped with the proper accessories, from the alternator to the air conditioning pump, power steering pumps, fuel filters, transmission, coolant recovery tanks, and any other accessories that the customer

has specified. We offer Cummins, Detroit Diesel, and Caterpillar engines with horse-powers up to 500. ②

During the chassis assembly, several processes are happening at the same time. While the engine is being moved to the chassis frame for installation, the cab is being trimmed to the customer's specifications. At KME we offer over 200 different cab configurations for our custom chassis. And we build them with three different materials: stainless steel, galvanized steel, and aluminum. We offer a wide variety of seating arrangements, both forward-facing and rear-facing, and several different roof types are available on any cab design. For the upholstery in our KME trucks, we use rolled and pleated Naugahyde on the door panels. We also have a molded door panel assembly available. ③

Fire departments put a lot of pride into their trucks, not only in how shiny they are on the outside but how shiny they are on the inside and underneath. It's very common here at KME to paint the frame rails one color and add a contrasting color to the cab. ④

As the chassis frame and engine assembly is completed, the cab is then installed on the truck and all the accessories in the cab are wired to the chassis. Today's fire trucks have a lot of creature comforts, everything from air-ride seats to tilt and telescoping steering columns. This particular truck has a video camera on it, so the driver can see what's happening behind the vehicle. ⑤

The company's world headquarters is in Nesquehoning, PA, on a 65-acre complex. The facility includes 11 plants with more than 500,000 square feet under one roof.

While the chassis is out on road test, the body for that chassis is being welded together. We make bodies here for rescue trucks, aerials, and pumpers, and we make them out of three different metals, the same as the cab. We can make aluminum, galvanized-steel, or stainless-steel bodies. After the body has been welded, it gets metal-fitted. In this area we're metal-fitting the body and getting it ready for a third coat of primer and rust-proofing. ⑥

All cabs and bodies at KME go through a paint process developed by PPG. That involves cleaning the material, a prime coat, a rust-proofing coat, and a finish coat of paint. At KME all of our major components are fully painted before we put them on the vehicle to ensure proper paint coverage all around the vehicle. All of our paint is to the customer's specifications and the customer's color.

This is a custom KME rescue body being installed on an International 4900 chassis. ⑦ The rescue body has been designed to the customer's specifications. After the body is installed on a chassis, the chassis will leave this area and go over to a finish area where all of the accessories will be mounted on the truck.

Next we come to our plumbing area, where we configure the fire pump on the truck. At KME the plumbing on our trucks is engineered to the customer's specifications. In this particular case, the customer wanted a manifold. This truck has a foam system on it, utilizing a Hale pump and Hale foam pro system. Hale is our primary manufacturer of fire pumps. They're based in Conshohocken, PA, and are the leading manufacturer of fire pumps in the United States. (8)

The company's newest division is Kovatch Mobile Equipment's Airport Products Group, which provides specialty vehicles to the airport market. The products include airport snowplows, pusher chassis, and aircraft refuelers.

At KME all of our lettering is computer-generated. This particular truck is getting simulated gold leaf applied, and in the event of damage it could be easily reproduced here at the factory and sent out to be installed in the field. (9)

In this area we're doing pump panel buildup prior to installation on the trucks. (10) Pump panels are designed on AutoCAD. They're fabricated and then assembled to the customer's specifications as to where they want the location of their gauges, their controls, and the valving that goes behind the pump panel. All pump panels are hinged for easy maintenance out in the field.

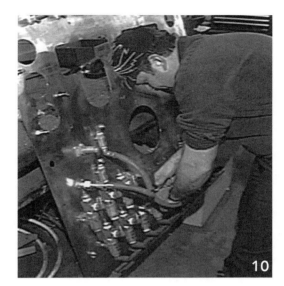

We're inside a command module area of a new KME pumper. This particular truck has a 2,000-gallon-a-minute pump. The advantage of this truck is that the operator of the pump could be inside and elevated where he has a good view of the whole fire scene, and yet he's off the ground and away from any obstructions. (11)

This is a KME custom pumper being completed for Lake Tahoe, NV. It has a four-wheel-drive chassis and a 1,500-gallon-per-minute pump with a compressed air foam

system on it. Compressed air foam systems are unique. They put out a foam that's similar to shaving cream and they can blanket a large area or a house or a building in a very short period of time. (12)

The business was founded by John "Sonny" Kovatch, Jr., who returned from World War II and opened a small, two-car repair shop. Today the company is the largest privately held manufacturer of fire trucks in the country.

With units recently delivered in Central and South America, Africa, and the Middle East, KME fire engines are more and more being used around the world. In 1999, nine units were delivered to Bosnia and 12 units were delivered to Kosovo, Yugoslavia.

It is common practice at KME that as the trucks are being completed, customers are here doing inspections on their vehicle. This is a new KME chassis and body for the City of Philadelphia, with a refurbished snorkel on it. It is one of three that we have built for Philadelphia. ⑬

Several times during the tour I mentioned custom fire apparatus and customers' specifications. That's what we're about here at KME: building custom fire apparatus to the customer's specifications. We're very proud of our product and we are a leader in the industry.

13

Location	Mack Trucks, Inc.
	7000 Alburtis Road
	Macungie, PA 18062
	(610) 709-3011
	www.macktrucks.com
Hours	Public tours available Tuesday and Friday, 8:00 a.m. to 1:00 p.m. Tours must be scheduled in advance.
	Museum open Monday, Wednesday, and Friday, 10:00 a.m. to 4:00 p.m. Call before visiting the museum.
	Rated as one of the top 10 places to visit by *USA Today*.
Tour Guide	Tom Kelly
	Vice President—Marketing

Mack Trucks, Inc., is headquartered in Allentown, PA, and the Macungie plant is one of its North American assembly facilities. This particular facility builds Class 8 trucks. We're going to be touring the H line as well as its supporting assembly operation that enables us to build those Class 8 trucks.

We want to start with the frame that comes from a supplier by the name of Dana from Lancaster, PA, who builds these frames for Mack. They arrive here in sequence to the production schedule. We'll be heading over to the beginning of the H line, where those frames are first introduced in our production process. ①

This frame is moving into position on the H line to begin the assembly process. This is an area we call the rough side of the H chassis line. Here is where we start to assemble the components of the chassis. Each truck on this line will be unique and have its own set of specifications and configurations.

We have approximately 200 different configurations of air tanks, for example, which are customized to fit a given customer's specifications.

Here we see an employee routing lines inside the frame. This is a very detailed operation, which must be done properly to ensure vehicle quality. Our intent is to keep any line from rubbing against any other component to prevent chafing of that line and premature failure of a component. ②

The average age of the workers here at the plant is 48 to 50 years old. Most employees are highly experienced and have been building trucks for 20 to 25 years.

Here we see additional components being attached to the truck. We use air tools to do most of the assembly work. You'll notice an awful lot of bolts that are used in the assembly operations, but that provides strength and rigidity. ③

Building the truck along an assembly line allows us to get into places on the truck for assembly purposes that would be difficult to do otherwise. It allows for the

workers to be properly positioned to attach various components. We use hardware that ranges from very small to very large in assembling the truck. A truck is in station approximately 20 minutes at the speed we're running the line. This allows a group of employees to attach a predefined set of components to that truck in accordance with its specifications.

In this operation we're attaching the bumper to the truck. ④ We have about 200 different varieties of bumpers that are attached to a truck to fit customers' specifications. Again, we're in the business of providing the customer with a customized, specific tool for his particular needs.

Upon completion of this task, the truck continues along the assembly line, progressing toward the chassis paint booth, where we will apply a color to that chassis as a rust preventative. Sometimes we do custom colors for the chassis because in the Class 8 business, the color of a truck is many times that customer's business trademark. So the color is very important to the customer.

As we progress down toward the chassis spray booth, you'll see two sprayers working. In this particular application they're spraying a chassis with black paint, which will provide a nice sheen to the truck. ⑤

In 1900, three brothers—Jack, Augustus, and William Mack—founded the company, originally called the Mack Brothers Company. Their first vehicle was a bus, used for touring Brooklyn's Prospect Park.

Mack Brothers Motor Car Company began production in Allentown, PA, in 1905.

We're progressing toward what we call the engine mounting area. We're going to observe the mating of the engine and the transmission, which are both produced at Mack's Hagerstown, MD, facility.

This operation requires great teamwork and skill. It's very sophisticated, and similar to the docking that occurs on the space shuttle system. Coordination and a proper attachment of all bolts is necessary to ensure the quality of the vehicle. It's extremely heavy componentry, and we use various cranes and hoists in order to make the attachment of these two units as easy as possible. ⑥

A very familiar component, which has just been attached, is the fan drive piece. It's very similar to a car engine, and we also use fan drive on our engines. As with all our vehicles, this particular engine configuration has a different fan drive, as specified by the customer. This again represents a type or variety that we run into on a daily basis in our assembly operations. ⑦

On this particular line, we trim out approximately 48 engines and transmissions each day. The engines were hot-tested in Hagerstown, MD, before the assembly. The engines won't be started here until after they're assembled into the trucks on the H line.

This is a finished, trimmed engine and transmission assembly being dropped inside the truck frame. ⑧ This operation is critical. It requires a great deal of teamwork and coordination in terms of handling the engine and transmission as well as attaching it to the frame. Everything has to be timed properly and done in the proper sequence.

The employees who work at this particular operation have been doing this a number of years and are highly skilled. At the same time they are doing this, the assembly line is moving forward. It adds a degree of difficulty to the operation, but we have the start of another successful mounting. We now have the real heart of the truck put in place.

We've now moved to the paint area, which is really the start of the cab line. We have approximately 4,500 different colors that are applied to trucks. We can see this employee spray-painting or applying clear coat to a tri-colored cab, which is halfway down the line. The employees are protected by environmental hoods with fresh air pumped through the hoods. So they are fairly comfortable while painting. ⑨

Next we come to the area where we mount the lights and the horn on the roof of the cab. We commonly refer to them as bullet lights. These bullet lights have become closely associated with Mack. We have customers

who prefer this type of light to some of the contemporary designs, as they believe it enhances the truck's image. It is part of the Mack culture and Mack character. ⑩

In this particular truck we're going to see the heater/air conditioner unit being installed inside the cab. It's a separate box, and it will be mounted in the center of the dash and become part of that truck. The employee has to position himself properly in order to prevent any possible strains and aches. This type of operation represents the heart of the assembly process, which is: a given employee completing a given set of assigned tasks in a specific time frame for a given chassis. That's how we organize the work along the line. ⑪

Next we see the windshield being installed. ⑫ The employee applies a lubricant to allow the windshield to slide in smoothly without breakage and to form a very tight seal. He uses a specifically designed tool to accomplish this task. We match it to the design of the rubber molding around that windshield.

Next we will see a cab being put into position to be mounted to the next chassis on the assembly line. ⑬ This is a very critical operation, requiring at least as much teamwork as mounting the engine transmission on the truck. This cab is a conventional, which means this truck will also get a hood, which will cover the engine. Our employees will be very careful positioning this as they try to hit the cab mounts dead

on. It's being guided from both sides by six employees, and it looks like they're pretty much on target. The hoist is then relaxed and the employees proceed with all of the attachments in order to fasten this cab to this chassis.

The next operation is where one of the most important parts of the truck is mounted—the Mack bulldog symbol. This symbol was designed in 1932 by a Mack engineer, and has been used ever since. It has become a critical part of the trademark for Mack. It's a rather simple operation but a very important one that customers have come to expect. We use a variety of bulldogs, including some gold or gold-colored bulldogs. (14)

We'll now move down the assembly line to the tire-mounting station. In this particular case we are using aluminum rims, which are a more high-appearance item. An employee can rotate a tire of this size with one hand because of the roller conveyors

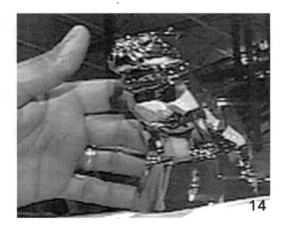

supporting that tire. It's another specialized piece of equipment in the assembly process. This operation is being done simultaneously on both sides of the line. Next we'll attach the lugs. During this operation great care is taken not to scratch the surface of the rims. Customers take a great deal of pride in the appearance of their truck; it is where they spend a substantial portion of their workday. (15)

The company became associated with the bulldog during World War I, when the British government purchased the Mack AC model to supply its front lines. British soldiers called the truck the "Bulldog Mack," because its shape and durability reminded them of the country's mascot, the British bulldog.

15

The unit you see here was just started up for the first time. (16) This model is an RD and most likely will get a dump body put on the back of it. Almost all of the trucks at this plant will end up having some type of body put on them, whether it be a barrel for cement mixers, a dump truck body, or even possibly a van body.

The truck is now ready to be driven off. But first we'll do a quick check on the final specifications, an adjustment of the mirrors, and a sounding of the horn. The horn signals the truck is coming off the line, and off the line it comes. The truck will now be dynamometer-tested and go through a final set of adjustments before shipment to the customer.

16

Malmark
BELLCRAFTSMEN

Location	Malmark Bellcraftsmen
	Bell Crest Park
	P.O. Box 1200
	Plumsteadville, PA 18949
	(215) 766-7200
	www.malmark.com
Hours	Public tours available Monday through Friday, 8:00 a.m. to 3:30 p.m., by appointment only.
Tour Guide	Jacob Malta
	President

Welcome to Malmark, America's premier bell craftsmen. We are one of two hand-bell producers in the Western Hemisphere, and one of five in the whole world. We devote our full-time talents and facilities to the design and crafting of fine English handbells, choral chime instruments, and a complete line of ringing accessories. We serve handbell choirs and ringing groups in churches, schools, and organizations throughout the world. ①

Let's look first at a very important part of this operation. On the following page you see our masters. ② All of these are castings, which I developed over the years. Many thousands of hours were involved in creating these. They are the masters for every bell that we make, and the machinists make reference to the readings that I've written on them. They use these to set up their machines.

In the machine shop, a lathe is being operated to turn the OD, the outside diameter of the bell. We have a cutting tool on the end of the tool hold-

er, and it's going to engage the stem, or tang, on the bell and start to remove metal somewhere along the line. The bell is made from a sand casting, and sand castings are never uniform because the sand in the mold compresses unevenly. So during the first cuts it may cut in certain areas on one bell and in other areas on the next bell. ③

This device is a hydraulic tracer. ④ It contains a hydraulic cylinder, which is controlled by a stylus. The stylus has a large diameter, which is now in contact with the template, and the diameter reduces as it goes up. On the template you can see the outside shape of the bell. Every bell that we turn has to have an outside template such as this.

This tracer has completed its first cut and has come back in about a third of the way through its second cut. In a few seconds it'll complete this cut and it will reverse itself automatically. As you can see on this second cut, it has completely removed the outer skin of the casting. There are times when you go through three cuts before it will do that. Again, it's just because of the fact that sand castings are never uniform with respect to each other. ⑤

We don't throw away the shavings, those chips that come off the bells as we turn them. They are extremely valuable. We have to pay the foundry $7 to $8 per pound for castings. So we save all these chips, and when we accumulate 30,000 to 40,000 pounds, a truck will come in and pick up the entire shipment, and take it to Chicago, where it's reprocessed. It's melted down in furnaces, the alloy content is checked and corrected, and then it's poured into bars, which they return to us, and we then distribute them to the foundries. ⑥

In 1984, Malmark introduced the world's first seven-octave set of handbells at a concert given by Westminster Choir College of Princeton, NJ.

The company now occupies a 42,000-square-foot plant and employs 60 people.

You saw on that first machine that we had a casting that was probably about 14 or 15 inches in diameter, and this here is one of our smallest bells. Just the size of a thimble. ⑦

In 1982, Malmark introduced its "Choir-chime" instruments to meet the demand for low-priced, high-quality handchimes for use in elementary music education. The company now manufactures more than 45,000 handbells and 75,000 Choirchimes each year.

The tone this bell makes is referred to as a C9. That is a note that is way above the highest note on a piano keyboard. So it gives you an idea of the range of bells that Malmark makes.

Next we come to the polishing and sanding department, where we've got six different operators working, sanding the inside of the bells. One operator has just finished sanding, and now he is using a flexible shaft machine. ⑧ There's a polishing bob on the end of it, and the flexible shaft is turning at about 3,450 revolutions per minute. At the same time, the bell is turning at 3,450 revolutions per minute in the opposite direction. So we've got nearly 7,000 RPMs working for us in producing a high polish on the inside of the bell. That develops a great deal of friction and a great deal of heat. It's necessary for him to read the frequency of the bell to make sure it is producing the correct tone before he passes the bell on for outside polishing. So he's got to allow that bell to cool before it's read. He is attempting to get all the tooling marks off the inside of the bell, and to bring the bell down to the correct pitch.

Malmark was incorporated in December 1973 by Jacob Malta. He previously served as vice president and chief engineer for Schulmerich Carillons, Inc., of Sellersville, PA.

What we have here is an outside polishing operation. ⑨ After the bells have been polished on the inside, they're brought over here. This operator is holding a bell and rotating it by means of handles, and he's holding it against the high-speed polishing wheel. He just applied a tritoli compound, which is the compound from which jeweler's polish is made, and he is removing all the machining and tooling marks from the outside of the bell. He goes around the entire surface, and when he's gone all the way around it, he inspects it visually to look for any film or blemishes that he hasn't polished over. When he is finished with the outside, he is going to refer to the chart, which tells him exactly the pitch the bell should be making, and if it doesn't read correctly, he just re-polishes. We purposely leave the bell higher in pitch—the thicker the bell, the higher the pitch—until we get down to the desired frequency.

Malmark opened its doors for business in May 1974. The first sets of 25 bells were shipped in the fall of that year.

Now I think I ought to show you what a clapper does to the sound of the bell—the variation that we can get from one clapper. ⑩ The clapper has four separate felt lobes on it, each with a different hardness. One makes a soft sound. The second lobe

is medium. It sounds like it's a different frequency, but the different lobe just changes the tonal color. In the third position you get an even more brilliant effect. So all of these felts are of a different density and will produce a different tonal quality when struck. The clapper settings can be changed during the course of playing a musical selection, and some composers write their music around that feature in our bells.

In a voicing room, the bells are not only rechecked as to frequencies, but they're also checked for mechanical defects. ⑪ They are also checked aurally; in other words, they are listened to. Even though the frequencies may be tuned correctly, the sound quality may not be acceptable. Each time our checker strikes that bell, each time her left hand touches it, she moves the casting in a circular fashion, just a very small amount. She just changed the clapper position from soft to medium to excite a higher frequency, which she's reading on the scope in front of her. Then she goes back and reads the fundamental frequency with the clapper in the soft position. She does that to find the best point of response on the bell. Now she's going to put a permanent scribe mark inside the bell in alignment with the plane in which the clapper moved. If in the future it's necessary to disassemble the bell to clean and polish it, it can be reassembled to that line again, which is the point of best response.

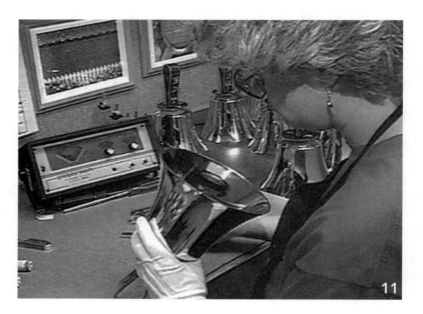

Our checker will reject a pretty large number of bells, probably about 20 percent of them, for sound-quality defects. Those that she rejects she sets aside and they must then go out to the final assembly tables and be disassembled. The one she just checked had an audible beat, a wow-wow-wow effect. That's what she's listening for in trying to locate a spot around the bell that produces a minimum of that effect.

Many of the bells that are rejected are set aside because they produce beats and wows. This is in addition to a fairly substantial number of bells rejected for surface defects. Here we have bells that have been completely assembled in the final assembly room, brought into the voicing department, been checked, and found lacking. ⑫ In other words, there are excessive beats and wows in them. They will not fit in with the standards of quality that we require in our bells. So these are all

rejects. With all of the cost and work done to them—turning, tuning, polishing, and voicing—this is, unfortunately, where an awful lot of bells end up.

In the shipping and receiving department the bells that pass inspection are prepared for shipment. Each bell is individually bagged and put into the appropriate pocket in the carrying case. Each pocket is marked with the musical note of the bell that fits into it. The case lid is padded, and when the lid is brought down, the padding in the lid holds the bell in the pocket. There's a pocket in the case in which there are items included in every shipment: a booklet of music, a polishing cloth, polish, and, of course, the guarantee. ⑬

Martin & Co.
EST. 1833

Location	C.F. Martin & Company 510 Sycamore Street Nazareth, PA 18064 (800) 633-2060 www.martinguitar.com
Hours	Public tours available Monday through Friday at 1:15 p.m. Museum open Monday through Friday, 8:00 a.m. to 5:00 p.m.
Tour Guide	Dick Boak Director of Marketing

The basic woods that we use on our guitars are mahogany and rosewood. There are two varieties of rosewood. Rosewood from Brazil is quite rare. Rosewood from India is the wood that we predominantly use. They are both very beautiful and tonally excellent. We also use curly maple, prominent in the United States and Germany, and curly koa. All of these woods are used for backs and sides on premium guitars, and they contribute to excellent tone. We use spruce from Oregon, Washington, British Columbia, and Alaska for braces as well as soundboards. ①

Among the other woods that we use is ebony for the fingerboard, a very good

material for durability and playability. We also use rosewood for fingerboards, and we use rosewood and ebony as well for bridges. The blocks of a guitar—the dovetail block, which accepts the neck, and the end block, which supports the bottom of the guitar—are made of mahogany. Spanish cedar, or cigar box or pencil cedar, is used for the interior lining of the guitar. It makes the guitar smell really nice.

Here we see the book-matching and inspecting of selections of

East Indian rosewood sets. ② A back is always book-matched from two pieces. The sides and top are done the same way. There are about 80 different shades of rosewood in any given tree, so we need to color-match the rosewood very carefully to make sure the sides and the back are matched as closely as possible.

2

After the wood has been inspected and selected for a particular model, the two halves of the top and back are carefully book-matched, and the seam is prepared and glued together on this unusual clamp carrier. ③ This tool is probably a hundred years old. This will enable us to get a very accurate seam for the back, as well as the top. These clamps actually keep the two halves of the back down while we clamp laterally with the other clamps.

3

The bracing is actually a fairly high-tech process that we've developed over the last 10 years. We used to glue the braces on with traditional hand clamps. This took a tremendous amount of time and effort. Over the last decade we developed a vacuum-clamping method that uses latex. On the next page you can see one of our workers applying glue to the braces and setting them into position. ④ She's now working on the famous Martin X-brace, which was invented by Martin, and copied by virtually every guitar maker in the world. All of these braces are as small as they can possibly be, so that the guitar is not over-braced, which would cause a bad, thick, muddy kind of sound. We also don't want the guitar to be under-braced because it would jeopardize the instrument, and possibly cause cracking.

The sides of the guitar are sanded to about 76 thousandths of an inch. That's quite thin, a little bit more than a sixteenth of an inch. In order to bend them, we heat these irons up to about 400 degrees, and they are very carefully bent by hand. This is an extremely skilled and difficult job. If you try to bend too hard, you can break the wood, and this wood is quite valuable. Sometimes, if the wood is a little

Prominent players of Martin guitars include Eric Clapton, Paul McCartney, Neil Young, Paul Simon, Jimmy Buffett, Joan Baez, Sting, Johnny Cash, Willie Nelson, and the Dixie Chicks. Martin players of the past include Hank Williams, Sr., Gene Autry, Elvis Presley, Elizabeth Cotton, Jimmie Rodgers, Lester Flatt, and Woody Guthrie.

Founder C.F. Martin was born in Germany in 1796, the son of a guitar maker. He came to America in 1833, and relocated his business from New York City to Nazareth, PA, about 1859.

obstinate or difficult to bend, we can spray it with water, which creates steam and aids in the bending process. And we have several different diameters of bending irons to achieve different radiuses of bends. (5)

Once the sides are bent, we take a dovetail block, cut it to accept the neck of the guitar, and stamp it with the model number and the serial number. Martin serial numbers are all sequential, so it shows the exact number of guitars we've built since we began to build this instrument. This is going to be a D28, and we've built slightly more than a half-million of these guitars since 1833. So the front block and the rear block are glued to the two halves of the sides, and this is what we call a rim. (6)

In addition to guitar-making, Martin is one of the world's largest manufacturers of musical strings, and a major distributor of fretted instrument accessories.

It would be almost impossible to glue a top or a back to this very thin sixteenth of an inch of side, and so we install ribbon lining onto the sides using a very low-tech approach—clothespins. ⑦ This gives us about a quarter of an inch of glue surface to attach the top and the back. The ribbon lining is made of Spanish cedar, the same type of cedar that you find in pencils and cigar boxes. It has a very attractive odor. The ribbon lining also has a tremendous amount to do with the tone of the guitar. It helps transfer the vibrations of the top and the back through the sides.

So once the ribbon lining is installed, the rim itself is complete, and we come back to the area where the braces are being shaped. After the braces have been shaped, the components of the top and the back are very carefully hand-fit. If you look closely at this work, you can see that our worker has done such a good job that you can't see any gap around the edges of the back braces. ⑧ That has been

C.F. Martin & Company is the oldest maker of guitars in the world, and the largest maker of acoustic guitars in the country. The company currently produces 225 guitars a day, totaling about 55,000 per year.

very carefully executed using very tiny pieces of ribbon lining, which have been cut into different widths. He inserts these pieces into small gaps, cuts them off with a razor knife, and sands them very clean. This is just part of the Martin philosophy. We want the inside of the guitar to be as flawless and as finely crafted as the outside.

Here we're working on one of the Eric Clapton models, and hand-fitting the neck to the body. (9) This is a very critical job. It's a very subtle neck angle, which is about a degree and a half back-pitch to the neck. It's critical to the playability and the string height of the guitar and its relation to the bridge. We use a number of templates to check the height of the bridge and the centering of the neck on the body. The dovetail of the neck has to be shaved as well to drop the neck into the body for a perfect fit.

After that the neck and body are given a code number, which enables them to be matched up at a later date. The two pieces will go through the entire sanding and finishing process separately, and are matched up at the very end after lacquering.

After the neck has been fit to the body, the neck can then be shaped with a draw knife. (10) The draw knife is actually a tool that was used to shape wagon wheel spokes during the colonial days. When Mr. Martin moved to the United States, this tool made perfect sense for carving necks. It enables the neck carver to remove fairly substantial amounts of wood quickly and accurately.

After lacquering is complete, the guitar goes through several stages of polishing. This step requires several speeds of polishing and an assortment of different polishing compounds that are similar to the types of compounds that you would see in automobile polish. This requires a very delicate touch, because if we were to bear down too hard, we could break right through the finish to the raw wood. Once this process is done the guitar will have a beautiful mirror finish and the final polishing will be done by hand.

If you remember the neck shaper, the person who fit the neck to the body initially, he gave the neck a code number, which matches the body. There's no interchangeability after that point. The necks and bodies, after being completed in the polishing department, receive their tuning machines, and then, using the code numbers, we match up the two components. Then a very delicate final neck fit occurs, and small amounts of lacquer around the neck heel are removed. The neck fit is checked repeatedly to make sure that everything is flawless. Once it's determined that everything is just right, the neck is finally glued into place. (11)

After the bridge has gone into place, we string the guitars up for the first time. Stringing and tuning of the guitar also involves regulating and setting the saddle height and nut height, which determines how comfortable the instrument is to play. This is called "action." Most guitar players these days require lower and lower action because of the influence of the electric guitar. (12)

After final polishing the guitars come back for final inspection, and the inspectors are also our players. They check over every square inch of the instrument, making sure there are no scratches or any cosmetic problems, and also check over the neck and the playability. ⑬ And then there is only one thing left to do and that is to see how it plays. ⑭

Since 1833, Martin has produced more than 765,000 guitars.

Location	Mrs. T's Pierogies
	600 East Center Street
	Shenandoah, PA 17976
	(800) 233-3170
	www.pierogy.com
Hours	Public tours available by appointment,
	Monday through Friday, 8:00 a.m. to 4:00 p.m.
Tour Guide	Tim Twardzik
	Executive Vice President

Mrs. T's is the world's largest maker of pierogies. We have grown from a group of five people around my grandmother's kitchen table to more than 270 people working in two facilities. ①

The company was founded by my father, Ted, in 1952. He was inspired by his mother Mary's work with the local church groups in selling pierogies. Pierogy sales helped build a lot of the churches in our community. My dad graduated from college and worked for an accounting firm for about a year before he returned home and started making pierogies and selling them to the local stores. My brother and I joined my dad's business in the early 1980s. So we represent the second generation in the business.

We are a family-owned and -operated business here in Shenandoah and in East

Greenville, PA. Shenandoah is our world headquarters. That's where we have been operating since we were founded in 1952. As a matter of fact, this site is where we've been ever since my grandmother threw my dad out of the house, saying, "Stop making such a mess in my kitchen." We came down here to my grandfather Frank's bar when it was vacant, and we've been here ever since.

We are now making pierogies around the clock. We have grown from a couple of hundred dozen a week to over seven million pierogies a week. It's not a complicated task. A pierogy is a dough, and ours is a quality pasta sheet that we roll out. We cut circles out and fill them with a variety of fillings. The dough is folded over and pinched or crimped with a fork, and the product is then boiled. That's the traditional way of preparing it. So it's not complicated, but making the dough is a lot of hard work, and it's also very time-consuming.

The plant's bulk flour system consists of four bins holding 53,000 pounds of flour each. The flour was delivered here via tanker truck. It comes down in tubes and is distributed through the plant by a pneumatic system. This little "spaceship" sifter is used to eliminate any lumps and is a safety against foreign materials. ② It's much like the old-fashioned sifter your mother might have used at home, but it is able to keep up with our higher volumes. A series of magnets is also placed throughout our system, which guards against metal contamination. The bulk system has eliminated all our headaches, including dust and packaging waste, and improves our inventory controls. Sanitation is key here as it always is in a food plant, and having one central location for the major ingredients such as flour really keeps our plant cleaner. Here at Mrs. T's we use over 35,000 pounds of flour each day, 175,000 pounds of flour each week.

This container is a bulk egg tote. ③ It comes from Quaker State Farms in Pennsylvania. Buying eggs this way is wonderful for our production. They do the cracking for us, so instead of our having to prepare 2,000 pounds of eggs, which would work out to be over 20,000 fresh eggs, they do the work and put them in these containers. It's pasteurized so it works very well, and gives us a great quality. We have diced onions, again from a Pennsylvania manufacturer. These save us a lot

The company today employs 280 people, and is Shenandoah's largest employer. In 1996, Mrs. T's opened a second production facility in East Greenville, PA, which now employs 25 people.

of crying around the plant. They work well for our fresh potato and onion pierogies. We use a lot of dehydrated ingredients here because of the quality and consistency. Dehydrated onions come in 2,000-pound totes, which represent over 14,000 pounds of fresh onions, so again, it saves us a lot of warehousing space and gives us the quality control we need.

This cheese is dehydrated; it's real cheese with the water removed. Cheese is a food, so as it ages the flavor changes. By using dehydrated cheese, we can make the same quality product in January as we do in July. ④

We also use fresh cheese in our plant. Our American cheese comes to us in 40-pound blocks. Here we take our block and put it on this pneumatic slicer, which uses wires to cut the cheese into manageable blocks. The blocks are put into a shredder, making our fresh shredded cheese, which we use in our American cheese pierogies. ⑤

Mrs. T's Pierogies are sold from coast to coast in the U.S., and through U.S. military commissaries in Germany, Japan, and Okinawa.

Here we are in our potato station. Again, these come dehydrated for quality assurance. ⑥ Here we cut open the bags and pour them into the bulk transporting bin. When the kitchen staff needs to use the potato flakes, they simply push buttons on automatic weighing scales to deliver the correct amount of potatoes for each batch. Each bag of flakes represents over 280 pounds of fresh potatoes. We would need a plant many times as large as our present facility just to handle the potatoes themselves. We use approximately 50,000 pounds of potato flakes per week, the equivalent of 270,000 pounds of field potatoes.

Our next step will be going to the kitchen to mix some batches with filling and dough. After measuring our margarine to get the proper amount, we put it into a tilt brazier pan. The equipment you see here is very popular in restaurant kitchens, mass-feeding operations, and cruise lines. In a food plant the majority of the equipment is stainless steel, all government-approved. ⑦

Mary Twardzik, mother of company founder Ted Twardzik and grandmother of Tim Twardzik and company president Tom Twardzik, is the "Mrs. T" after whom the company is named. It is her recipe that forms the foundation of Mrs. T's Pierogies.

After this we place the fresh, chopped onions into our mix. We fry the onions to blend the flavors, and mix them into our filling. We blend our filling in commercial mixers. When our bowls are filled, we add our potatoes, our seasonings, and lastly our onions. We check the watering scale, which will meter the exact amount of water per batch. We now blend our real potatoes and rehydrate them with our water mixture, and this will give us a smooth, whipped potato.

We are now at our dough mixer. This large machine mixes in 400-pound batches. ⑧ We also have other machines that will mix up to 2,000-pound batches of dough. Here we will mix a new run of dough. First we draw flour into the system,

then we add pasteurized eggs and water, as the final ingredient, to the pasta dough. We blend warm and cold water to make sure the right temperature of water gets into the mix. It's an important step in the process of getting the right quality of dough every time. Next we turn on the mixer. We will mix the dough for the appointed time, and another batch of fresh pasta will turn into pierogies.

After it's been mixed, we pull out the dough and put it into the production area, where we have our top-secret machine that rolls and fills the pierogies and sends them on their way.

Now we find ourselves in our boiling room. Again, we can't show the top-secret machine that turns ingredients into pierogies, but the end result is coming off the conveyor belt. The pasta has been formed, we filled it with potatoes and cheese, and crimped the edges. They drop into a boiling tub and that precooks our pierogies. This way they won't fall apart for you at home. ⑨ After they go through the boiling tubs, they run onto a conveyor and transfer to a cooling area. Our cold-water tubs take the product, which is boiling, and cool it down to a temperature

Mrs. T's Pierogies have been available to students in Penn State University cafeterias since 1981. The students consume about 300,000 pierogies per year.

that is comfortable for our packing people. The cold-water bath removes the starch from the product and cools it at the same time. After the product cools, it is transferred to a packing table.

Here at Mrs. T's, every one of our pierogies is hand-inspected by quality staff. The product is picked up and placed in packages by hand. We put a sheet of poly in between the pierogies so they don't stick together. Our packers will pack between four and five boxes a minute. That's over 20,000 a day, three million a year. This is very labor-intensive, but it does give us an opportunity to check every one of the pierogies that goes out of our plant. The packers serve as our inspectors, and the number one rule is don't pack anything you wouldn't like to buy yourself. If it's not perfect, the pierogy is put into a bin and taken away to a food bank. We work with the Second Harvest Food Bank System. This program allows us to give back to our community. **(10)**

After the boxes are packaged, they make their trip up a conveyor belt to our pack-sealing equipment. These packages go into the sealing machine, where each box is coded with the production date and time so we know exactly who's done what, when, where, why, and how. **(11)**

Mrs. T's sponsors more than 120 athletic events each year, including the Mrs. T's Chicago Triathlon.

In the movie *Men in Black*, the last meal served to the head of the Arquillan Empire is Mrs. T's Pierogies.

After the packages are sealed, they continue on the conveyors to our next stop, which will be our freezers. These automatic-fed freezers were a big change in our operation. Instead of racks and trays and lifting, we now have computers, conveyors, and hydraulics to move the product through the freezers. The line feeds up to eleven packages, and a pusher arm will fill the trays one row at a time. As each tray is filled with product, the machine cycles and brings another empty tray to be filled. Once the entire system is filled, the freezer returns the first tray and starts all over again pushing the fresh product in and the frozen product out. A full freezer will hold over five tons of pierogies.

Automation has played a big role in getting our product into more and more markets as we've grown. We've been proud to grow our company, but never have people lost their jobs through automation. Our ink jet machine is computer-driven and it codes our production date, the time, and the case count so we can track all the products when they leave our plant. At the end of the line, they are placed on pallets and are almost ready to be shipped. ⑫

Next the pierogies enter their final resting place, at least here at Mrs. T's, which is our storage freezer. This freezer remains about 15 degrees below zero. When the pierogies leave Mrs. T's, they are shipped in refrigerated carriers to maintain their quality. In addition to our warehousing space, we use public warehousing throughout the country, from Chicago, to upstate New York, to Florida, to California. And yes, pierogies are even stored in lovely Hawaii, which is a nice change from the 15 degrees below zero of our freezer.

Orthey Instruments

Location	Orthey Instruments
	18 Burd Road
	Newport, PA 17074
	(717) 567-6406
	www.fmp.com/orthey
Hours	No public tours available.
Tour Guide	George Orthey

I'm Dr. George Orthey. I've lived here in Newport since 1955. My wife was from Newport from way back. Her eighth-generation grandparents settled in Landisburg, PA, in 1739, so our families have looked at this countryside for a long time. I would like to take you through my shop and a barn, show you some of the things that I do, and tell you something about the instruments that I make. ①

People say to me, "Do you do what you do from scratch?" And you're looking at "scratch" behind me. Scratch is the woods that you see back there. All the harps I make are made out of wood, and some of the wood that I use is cut from trees along the edge of the field over there. Some of the trees are Chinese chestnut trees, and

they give me some of the better-prized wood that I use. I've also cut several very large walnut trees out of my own woods to use on the instruments. So I don't know how you would get any "scratcher" than going down into the woods and cutting your own trees to build something.

After I cut down a tree, it has to be sawed and it has to be dried. It's necessary to quarter-saw wood for musical instruments. After it's sawed, the wood is wet and it's new, and you can't use wet new wood to build anything. You see in this pile the way the wood is set, with spacers in between, so that you get air circulation through it. ② The wood sits here for a

minimum of five years. If anything in that wood is going to cause it to warp and bend into unusual shapes, it would have happened before I get around to building the instrument. So I know that my wood will be stable and stay where it belongs when I'm finishing the instrument up.

I go through and sort and select the pieces that are useful. Just to give you an idea of what we end up with, I got a very large mulberry log from Joe Carter down in Virginia. He brought it up in his pickup truck. We estimated that it weighed 1,800 to 2,000 pounds, and by the time I got done sorting, taking out the pieces that were no good, cutting it, trimming it, and so on, what I had left that was perfectly useful to me I could pick up in my arms and carry at one time. That much wood left

from 1,800 pounds. So it is a very wasteful process to get the perfect wood that you need for musical instruments. But there's no use in making something that is not perfect.

I'll start out by showing you one of the instruments that I make. This is a commemorative Stoneman harp. It's made out of a Chinese chestnut tree that I talked about at the beginning of our tour. ③

On the following page you can see one of the basic patterns that I use. It shows me the position of my tuning pins. If you think about the harp we looked at, you can see the position of the tuning pins, and you see the position

of the bridges that the strings go across. ④ So I use this for my reference with each of the parts of the instrument as I put it together, and all of the pieces go together.

If you don't have a quality pattern that will make your instrument work, then you aren't going to come out at the right place, and you'll find halfway through that the stuff won't go together right. If you do that, then you have to start all over again from scratch.

The frame is made of hard-rock sugar maple. You can see the lamination in this. It's piano pin block. It's made for putting the tuning pins on the inside of a piano. It's very strong. Since it is a plywood there's no chance for it to split. The pins are going to hold tight, and will remain tight for years and years and years. The other parts of the frame are not laminated. They are straight sugar maple. ⑤

Now we start seeing it take some kind of configuration, but again I have to use my pattern. You may have noticed in the Pop Stoneman commemorative harp I showed you earlier that it has a sound hole with a daisy or flower shape to it. So I use this pattern, which lets me draw my flower like that. ⑥

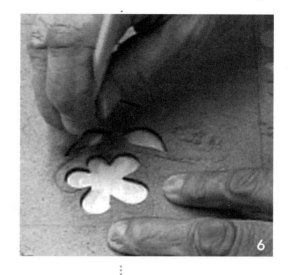

Now we're going to put the soundboard braces on. I'm making some marks here to give me a guide for where my braces go. They are on the inside of the soundboard. ⑦

Next I'll take a pattern and put it on the back of the instrument, and I mark the edges so that I know where it goes. And being a bright boy, I mark it with a B, which tells me that's the back. So the braces are inside of the back, and are cut into the frame so that everything lies smooth and flat. That gives us our top soundboard and our back.

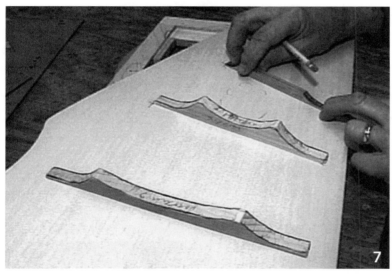

Among the many performers who play Orthey instruments are Bryan Bowers, June Carter Cash, John Sebastian, Mike Seeger, Peggy Seeger, Patsy Stoneman, and Doc Watson.

Let me tell you about some of the machinery that I use to do this. First I use a joiner, which makes a clean edge on the wood. Next I go over to my table saw. Earlier I said how wasteful this process is. I've already taken this piece of board and I've just thrown away 30 percent of it. So here goes another stage of the wastefulness. Then I take this on my big band saw and I resaw it to make pieces for the back of the instrument. You've always got to be careful with these saws if you like your fingers. After 36 years of instrument-making, I've still got all ten fingers. ⑧

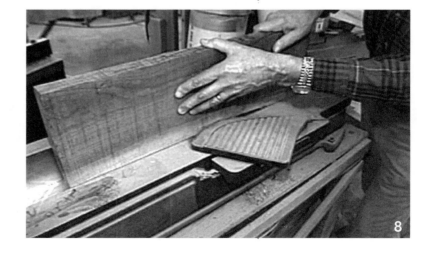

I use the band saw to cut the wood in half, and when I open it up, it makes what we call a book-matched pattern.

All totaled, Orthey
Instruments has
produced two guitars,
over 100 hammer
dulcimers, plucked
psalteries, and bowed
psalteries, and 1,639
Appalachian dulcimers.
Since 1984, Dr. Orthey
has dedicated himself
exclusively to making
autoharps.

Those two pieces of wood are from right next to each other. Then I glue these two pieces together, and if you don't do that—if you use a piece of wood from here on one board and a piece from there on another board—when you play that instrument, the sound of the strings over on this part of the instrument will be different from the sound of the strings over on that part of the instrument. So the pieces always have to be matched like this. ⑨

After I have sanded it down to the correct thickness, I cut out the piece from my pattern. This is curly wood. When you tip it back and forth to the light, you can see a pattern change in it, because it has these stripes in the wood. Of course, when you book-match it all together, it makes a very nice-looking finished back. ⑩

Next we have to build the chord bars. All of this cutting reminds me of a butcher slicing ham. You can see that after I am finished cutting the bars, the pattern of the grain is still there in those pieces. So when they go on the finished instrument, you can clearly see the grain and the color. ⑪

When I do chord bars, I usually set up and do nothing else for maybe a month. The last time I made chord bars, I made around 2,800 of them, and I don't have to do that again for two or three years. I call it my turnips. You know when you have to eat turnips. You get them all on your plate at one time and eat them and get it over with.

The string sets for the autoharp come in standard sets of 36 or 37 strings, depending on the instrument. This string is going into a fine tuner. ⑫ You see the way that little cam is rotating back to the right makes the string tighter. I turn it the other way and it comes back. That gives you fine tuning so you can tune the string exactly. At the top end of the harp you tune with tuning pins, and the tuning pins are much more difficult to get exactly where you want, especially when you have real short strings. When you have real short strings, they're hard to get in tune. The shorter the string gets, the more it changes with a little tiny movement of the tuning pin.

I'm just taking my tuning pin and I'm going to bang on it and drive it right in. There, I missed a little bit there and hit my finger. ⑬ You always put your fingers on the side of the tuning pin because you don't want to dent the instrument. Besides, it's painful when you hit your finger like that, and it teaches you to be more careful the next time. Then after I get all of the strings onto the instrument, I tune it up immediately. You never leave an instrument like this untuned. A string is like a lost cat; it always tries to find its way back home. If you put this instrument aside and get it out six months from now, you will tune it, and tune it, and tune it, and the strings will keep trying to go back to where they were when they were all wrong. So when I finish getting the strings on this, I immediately tune the instrument up so that I'm establishing in the memory of those strings where they should be, not where they are when in error.

All of my life I've enjoyed the kind of music that we do, and it has nothing to do with what I did in the real world. I was a veterinarian in the real world. But I enjoy the old-time music, and making the instruments introduces me to the people who play it, and lets me join with them in the joy of this instrument. ⑭

PENNSYLVANIA HOUSE

Location	Pennsylvania House 137 North 10th Street Lewisburg, PA 17837 (570) 523-1285 www.pennsylvaniahouse.com
Hours	No public tours available.
Tour Guide	Ken Fonville

Pennsylvania House Furniture is located here in Lewisburg, PA, in the heart of the Susquehanna Valley. We're about halfway between Harrisburg and Williamsport. We have been located here since 1889, when the company was founded as the Lewisburg Chair Factory to make cane-bottom chairs, which were very popular at the end of the Victorian era. We have had generations of workers here at Pennsylvania House making furniture for the last 100 years. ①

We're going to begin our tour in the lumberyard. We have stored here, most of the time, about three million board-feet of lumber. Most of it is Appalachian cherry, which comes from the forest right around us and through western New York state and West Virginia. We also work in oak, maple, and pine—all three good American woods.

When lumber is harvested, the natural moisture content ranges from 35 to 70 percent water. As the

lumber is brought here to our lumberyard, we leave it outside to allow it to dry naturally. Then we put it into a building called a pre-dryer to even out the moisture in the wood. The lumber is then placed in what is called a dry kiln. The kiln is a large enclosed area where the lumber is given applications of heat and humidity to bring it to a moisture content of about 5 to 6 percent.

After the lumber has been dried, it is brought into what's called the scaling shed. ② This is where we grade the lumber as it comes from the mill to us. Each stack of lumber comes across this conveyor belt in front of us and goes through a planer where it's evened up, and the roughness is taken out of the boards. That enables the grader to see any defects in the lumber. As it comes out of the planer, it goes onto another conveyor belt where the lumber grader evaluates the pieces, throwing out the ones that are defective.

This is the ripping operation. ③ One of the things that is unique about using wood as a raw material is that there are hidden stresses and strains inside the wood that were created as the tree grew in the forest. We relieve those stresses by cutting

the wood into thinner strips and then gluing it back together, which makes a stronger board for use in manufacturing. So here the operators cut the boards into thinner strips. They also cut out defects like knots and pieces of bark at this point as well. You see the operator throwing the scrap into an overhead conveyor line. All of the scrap in the plant, both these pieces and the sawdust that gets generated by sanding and by other cutting operations, is recycled. It goes into a silo where we cut it all into sawdust, and then that sawdust is used to fire the boilers that heat the plant, heat the dry kilns, and generate electricity. That allows us to be very efficient and not have a great deal of waste that has to go to a landfill.

At this point for the first time you see the pieces of lumber beginning to look like furniture parts. In this operation the individual strips of wood are put on a track. Once the strips are created, they pass over a gluing wheel, and the operator lays up the glued panels. What you're seeing now is the last panel getting ready to come off the gluing clamp. ④

After this comes the planing and sanding operation. Once the panels are glued, it's important for them to have a very specific size and thickness. We use wide-belt sanders where the panel goes through a rough cutting and sanding operation, and then through a second finer belt that gives us a very smooth surface to work with.

One of the other things that I might mention at this point is that the temperature and the humidity are very specifically controlled in the entire plant. As you walk around the plant, you will see steam generators that put humidity in the air, and a lot of fans that keep the air moving so the temperature and humidity remain very stable. This is because we don't want the wood to move once we have it as dry as we want it.

One of our newest pieces of equipment is a computerized work center. It does several operations automatically. The fact that it's controlled by the computer means that we don't produce as much scrap, and it doesn't require setup pieces for adjusting the machine. The panels are held down to this table by vacuum pressure, and the multiple heads will do many operations at the same time. This is a headboard panel that we're doing. ⑤ First the machine cuts the holes for screw applications; it then changes heads and begins to cut out the shape of the headboard. So what was a square piece of wood 30 seconds ago is now an almost finished part, ready to go to the assembly area.

One of the last operations in the parts-making process is to put a fine sanding on every piece before it goes to assembly. Here you see an automated sanding process that sands the shape on the edge of a dining table. ⑥ Here we sand the dinner table halves and the table leaves at the same time so the shapes will match perfectly in your table at home. These parts are then kept together throughout the rest of the manufacturing process so that they will always match. When you get a Pennsylvania House table, if you look underneath, you will always see a number. And the number on the table half will match the number on the table leaf.

In the assembly part of the plant, it's a little quieter since we've gotten away from the big, heavy machines that you saw in the front of the plant.

Here you see a craftsman doing a drawer assembly. ⑦ All the drawer parts that were machined downstairs have now been moved up here so that we can

assemble each drawer. Once in a while we have a problem with a part, and this is a good place to catch it, because it then doesn't go into the furniture. We take the drawer front and the two drawer sides, glue them in place, and then assemble the back and the bottom. It's clamped up to make sure that it's square and all of the joints are tight. On the bottom we use a jig to locate the wooden drawer guide and staple it in place. The final operation is to install what are called glue blocks that are designed to keep the parts square and to prevent the drawer bottom from rattling. Then the drawer bottom is set aside to go down to the rest of the

assembly cell for assembly into a finished case. As you can see, we assemble a great many drawers in the course of a day.

One of the things that's unique to Pennsylvania House, among all furniture manufacturers, is that we use a process called cellular assembly. Instead of a long assembly line like you're used to seeing in an automobile plant, we have small teams that are dedicated to making specific kinds of furniture. So what you're watching is the beginning of a dresser being made in a cell that is composed of about eight different people. This team works together every day, and they're paid based not only on their output, but on maintaining quality levels. ⑧

The subassemblies that you saw being made earlier are brought together in this area, and the original pieces are put together in a large clamp to ensure that the case is square. So the clamp maintains the quality and the size of each piece. After the case is preassembled with the glue, it's put in the clamp, and then the final operations are done there while the clamp maintains the structural integrity of the case.

After the case carcasses are assembled, they are moved to the next station, where the case fitters put in the drawers and doors and all those kinds of things. You're seeing here an example of one of the features of cellular assembly, in that

Pennsylvania House produces more than 200,000 wood products each year, and distributes them primarily through furniture and department stores.

you are watching the case fitters attaching the top to one type of case, called an armoire, and right behind it on the line is another type of case, a dresser, that will be the next piece they assemble. (9) This quick conversion from one case to another is one of the special attractions of cellular assembly. As you can also see, the case tops and backs in our product are plywood rather than cardboard or some other material. This adds to the structural integrity as well as the solid-wood nature of the product we manufacture.

What you're looking at is a china deck that is beginning to be processed. (10) You see the construction of the crown and the frame has been put together, and now glue blocks are put in to ensure that the pieces remain perpendicular and stay in place through shipping and for years to come in your home.

Once the doors are installed, this case gets a final inspection by the people who put it together. So in the space of about 30 feet the case has been completely assembled and inspected, and is now ready to go to the finishing line. We have cells like this that specialize in china decks, in dressers, tables, chairs, night stands, wall system pieces, and entertainment centers. Each of the different kinds of furniture that we make has a specialized assembly team that manufactures it every day.

Thus far you've seen many examples of the fine craftsmanship that it takes to manufacture Pennsylvania House furniture. From this point on, you'll see examples of the artistry that's associated with creating the fine finish of our furniture. You're at both the beginning and the end of the finishing line. ⑪ The raw cases from the staging area will go down a row and into the finishing booths. When they come back to this area, they go to the final inspection and a repair station before they go downstairs to have their hardware and glass applied.

One of the things about finishing fine furniture is that it takes many, many steps and applications of materials to the piece. After the furniture receives what we call a cap stain or equalizing stain, the piece gets a coating of what's called a sanding sealer, so that it ties down the color that's been applied and helps seal the surface before we apply the other coats.

This is the next color application stage, and it's the beginning of a very labor-intensive part of the process. ⑫ This is the color glaze that is applied to the case

The company now has more than 700 employees at the Lewisburg and White Deer plants in Pennsylvania, with a total plant size of 640,000 square feet.

in a very heavy manner by the spray operator. It's then wiped off to achieve the appropriate color. At this point in the process all of the cases are very dark and very dull. It's only later that they'll begin to acquire the high sheen and fine finish that you associate with Pennsylvania House. But as you see, there is a great deal of effort involved in applying these base coats of color for the richness, the depth, and the clarity that we are trying to achieve in all of our furniture. The operator working on this china deck puts as much finish on the back of the piece, the parts that you don't see, as he does on the parts that you do see. That's to make sure that the piece is very stable and doesn't have any unequal moisture content in it, so that it will stay stable in your home.

Here you see the glaze wipers at work. ⑬ This process begins to put the unique flavor and individuality into each piece. As the glaze wipers wipe off that heavy coat of glaze you saw being applied earlier, they also use the rag to begin to accentuate the grain and create the richness and clarity associated with a Pennsylvania House finish. Once these operations are finished, the case goes on the track for an extended period of time to allow it to dry completely before the next applications are put on the case.

13

After all of the color coats have been applied, the next step is to apply a coat of clear sealer. Then after that is done, we do a light sanding over the entire piece. This sealer sanding is one of the ways in which we get a very smooth finish that feels good when you touch it. So the entire piece is completely sanded and wiped down with a tack rag to get the sanding dust off before it gets the clear coats or the lacquer coats that provide the top layer of finish.

Here you see the first of typically three lacquer coats that go on. You can see the beauty of each individual piece begin to emerge as the lacquers free up the color and expose the beauty of the wood that heretofore has been concealed by the heaviness of the stains. We apply multiple coats of lacquer and sand between each one to ensure that it goes on smoothly and that we get even coverage. This gives a surface, which we will rub by hand or by machine to get the smoothness, the depth, and the clarity. ⑭

After the final lacquer has been applied, all of the cases go into a long oven. This oven is fueled by the sawdust and scraps that you saw when we began the tour. The oven allows the lacquers and the finishing materials to dry completely and to begin the curing process before they're packed for shipment.

Dining tables get very special attention here at Pennsylvania House. Every dining table is allowed to dry overnight so that the lacquer gets especially hard. Then we use these 30-pound rubbing machines to get a very even surface on the table top. ⑮ The rubbing compound is applied with a number of different levels of cutting paper to reliquefy the lacquer slightly and create a very smooth finish to the table top. This is how we get the fine finish that looks like it's a foot deep when you look down into your dining-table top. This operator has used a number of grits of paper to progressively polish the top of the table.

After the machine rubbing operation, a fine combination of wax and cleaner is hand-applied to every table top, and every case top, for that matter. There's no substitute for the handwork necessary to get this fine finish. It really cannot be achieved in an automated way. All of these craftsmen have to know exactly what they're doing to know how much to rub, how hard to polish, and how much polish to apply to make sure that we get the finish that we're after without cutting through to the raw wood.

The brand name *Pennsylvania House* originated in 1933 with the Joseph Horne Department Store in Pittsburgh. The Lewisburg Chair Factory products, as they were then known, were displayed in a special area of the furniture floor in the downtown store.

After the piece has passed through final inspection, it comes down here to have the hardware and any glass or shelves added to it. Here you see the special rubber molding that's used to hold the glass in place. That gives it a very finished appearance, both on the inside and on the outside. Each piece of glass is carefully applied and the molding is cut to fit, so the glass is held in place without any rattles, and yet will withstand the rigors of shipment and everyday use.⑯

Well, that completes our tour of the manufacturing process here at Pennsylvania House. I hope you've enjoyed it. We are very proud to show it to you and we're very proud of the many craftsmen who have dedicated their lives to manufacturing solid-wood furniture out of the finest American hardwoods here in the Susquehanna Valley.⑰

Tour 16

PFALTZGRAFF

Location	The Pfaltzgraff Company 140 East Market Street York, PA 17401 (717) 848-5500 www.pfaltzgraff.com
Hours	Public tours available weekdays at 10:00 a.m., for ages 7 or older only. Reservations must be made at least one day ahead to schedule a guide.
Tour Guide	Fred Binderbush Vice President of Manufacturing

Our process begins when we receive our raw materials in clay form, by railcar, delivered to the rear of this complex. Behind us are a series of ten different silos where we store our raw materials when we receive them. Those materials are designed to be mixed together in our mixing operation, which is located above us. After mixing, the clay is practically ready to be used for production in its raw form.

Prior to that the clay will be passed through a vacuum chamber or pug mill where the air is removed. It's important to take air out of the clay, because air in the clay causes cracking during firing, along with other quality defects. ①

So we want to have an air-free clay product ready for the forming operation. Once that clay passes through the pug mill, it's ready to be turned into the shape of the piece being formed. Next we'll go to some of those forming areas to see how this clay is made into dinnerware items.

The first forming center that we're going to be visiting today is our ram press

1

operation. We use this method to form various accessory items such as serving dishes or kitchen accessories that are irregularly shaped. Our ram press operation is using the pug clay that's been prepared expressly for this item. In this case we're making a quiche dish. The clay used here is made especially for our bakeware items so the consumer has a high-quality item for oven and dishwasher use. ②

The clay is put in between the two dies and the operator presses the clay out into the shape. Through a purging process the clay is released from the porous dies. The die is wiped, and then we take off some of the rough edges that occur during the finishing process. This very wet piece of clay then goes into a dryer so that it can be handled, and some additional finishing processes can be completed for the item.

After the ware has passed through the dryer, it's ready to go through the finishing process, and that's basically a sponging operation. In this case we're using a semi-automatic machine that gets into the grooves of the clay and takes off some of that rough finished surface from the die. ③ After this, the piece is finished with a sponge, just to take off any light pieces of clay that may be on the surface. Then it goes through a final drying process before it's ready for glazing, which we'll see a little bit further in the process.

Next we'll go to our jiggering department. Jiggering is a different form of making articles of pottery, and is normally used to turn them into a round shape. Basically, we use machinery to recreate the potter's hands, instead of the potter using his hands to shape the inside and the outside of a piece. This equipment uses a plaster-of-paris bowl to form the exterior of the piece and a steel roller ball to form the interior of the piece. The turning or spinning operation turns the clay into the shape, and the excess clay is cut off. All of our clay at Pfaltzgraff is reprocessed and recy-

The Pfaltzgraff family of German immigrant potters began their company in 1811 in York, PA. The company remains family owned, and is headed by a fifth-generation member, Louis Appell, Jr.

The oldest continually operating pottery maker in the country, Pfaltzgraff today employs 2,300 people and occupies more than 1.3 million square feet of manufacturing and distribution facilities.

cled, with very little going to landfills to be disposed of. After the clay is formed into the shape of the piece, the entire mold goes into a dryer where 120-degree heat is applied so water can be taken out of the clay. ④

Next we'll look at our cup-making process. But before we can form a cup, we need to make the handles that are later attached to the cup. We form our handles by taking our clay material, putting it into a liquid form called slip, and pouring it into stacks of molds where the clay fills up the cavities of the molds. They next go through another drying process where the clay solidifies in the mold and later can be separated into individual handles. Here you see where the finished cast handles are being removed from the mold. ⑤

Now that the handles have been prepared, we're ready to form the cup. This process begins again with air-free clay being fed into the mold. The mold travels

down the line to the forming head, where the pieces turn into the final shape of the cup. The machine itself carries the mold through a dryer. Again at a relatively low temperature, the water is extracted from the clay into the mold and the clay begins to shrink in size. By the time it comes out of the dryer, the operator is able to lift the piece out of the mold and begin the finishing process in order to take some of the rough edges off of the rim. ⑥

After that, the operators use the handles that have been prepared and hand-apply them to the cups using what we call sticking slip. It's really clay, and it's made of the same material as the handle and the cup, but it's a very sticky substance. They apply a little bit to the edges of the handle and hand-apply the handle to the cup itself. After that the cup goes down the conveyor and through a drying process. ⑦

You may notice that the cups themselves seem larger than they appear in finished form. That's because our products shrink about 10 percent from the time they're made in the clay stage to the time they're fired in the kiln. So everything is designed in its mold state to be 10 percent larger than its finished state.

These cups are a part of our Hermitage pattern. This is a pattern that has been out on the market for more than 30 years, and it's still one of our largest-selling patterns. It's really a classic in the American domestic market. Now these cups go into a finishing dryer and are ready to be glazed.

Some of our items require a decorating step after finishing and before glazing, and this is an example of the banding that is done on a number of our items. This happens to be the Juniper cup that's being decorated. ⑧ The ink is being fed through lines down to brushes that apply the ink directly to the clay surface. These decorations are commonly found in the pottery industry, but are uniquely applied at Pfaltzgraff. And this underglaze decorating is really one of our specialties, which gives our product its unique look. Each product then, after being decorated at this step, is ready to be glazed in the next process.

Just like our clay materials, our glazes are all produced here at Pfaltzgraff. Glaze is actually a glass material, but it's prepared in a liquid form before it's fired. During the firing process this dry material turns into a glassy substrate that seals the pottery, and gives it its finished color.

This is our glazing department. Here in the Thomasville plant we use a carousel spray machine in order to apply the glaze over the surface of the ware. ⑨ The ware is loaded onto spinners. Then the carousel carries the ware into the glazing area,

where there are a number of separate nozzles or spray guns that are positioned in varying locations, with the objective of spraying a uniform coverage of glaze over the entire surface of the piece. The application is pretty complicated and critical at this point, because we're attempting to achieve a range of only a 10,000th to a 12,000th of an inch of glaze over the entire surface of the piece. So it's left up to the skilled operator to set the guns in such a way that we achieve that uniformity of application. As the pieces come out of this booth, they have a chance to dry briefly and then they go across a sponge belt. The sponge belt is a way of wiping the glaze off of the surface of the foot, or the bottom of the piece. We do this so that when we place the piece on the kiln car, the glaze will not fire onto the surface of the car. This ware then travels back down the line, goes onto trucks, and is ready to be taken over to the kiln for firing.

Our kilns are fired at 2,200 degrees Fahrenheit, and the objective here is to get a good, solid, dense load on the kiln car. And what we're trying to do is get a mix of ware on the kiln car in order to get good, stable firing during the process. At this point all the ware looks to be the same color, because all the glazes in their unfired state have a white appearance. But after kiln firing the pieces show their different colors. Our ceramic engineers have worked very hard to develop glazes that can all be fired at the same temperature, but result in a number of different colors. So we're able to load different colors of glazes all on the same kiln car during the same continuous firing. This kiln car will now travel through the kiln for a period of 8 to 12 hours, depending on the type of kiln. And during that time it will go through a very carefully controlled time and temperature curve to bring the ware up very slowly to the peak temperature. At the peak temperature the glaze and the clay mature, and they fuse together into a permanent bond. Then we control the cooling curve in such a way as to get the proper finish to the glaze. Some of our glazes have a shiny or glossy finish. Other glazes have a dull or mat finish. And the quality of the finish is determined in the cooling curve of the kiln. So temperature control is critical during the firing process so that we can achieve the uniformity and the quality of the product that our consumers expect. ⑩

We're now in the decorating part of the Thomasville operation. This is the area where, after we've done the first firing of the product, we apply additional decoration to some of the items that require a special decorating application. Some of our designs require brighter colors and details, and we use ceramic decals to apply those kinds of decorations. What you're seeing here is the hand application of some of the ceramic decals or transfers to the surface of the piece. ⑪ This is being applied to the glaze-fired surface. The process is one of soaking the decal off the gummed paper and moving it over to the ceramic surface. Then the decaller works to remove any water or air that might be trapped underneath the decal, so in a second firing process the color from the decal can be fired cleanly onto the surface of the glaze.

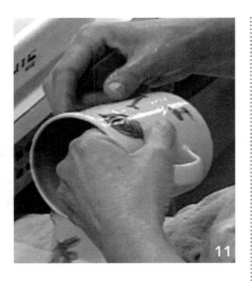

Here you can see we're decorating Naturewood mugs. An important part of the design is the decorations that are applied to the outside of the piece. After these pieces are decalled, they're assembled onto a kiln pallet, and that pallet will be taken out to the kiln to be fired in another operation.

Then we come to the final processing step for the decorated ware. It has now been decorated with the ceramic decals, and in some cases bands of color have been applied to the top edges of the rims. We use one of several kilns to fire the ceramic colors onto the surface of the glaze.

This is a continuously operating Lehr kiln, fired to 1,480 to 1,500 degrees Fahrenheit. At that temperature the colors in the ceramic decal again mature to their ceramic hardness and are permanently affixed to the glaze so that they are dishwasher- and oven-safe for use in your home. ⑫

The company's earliest pieces were jugs and crocks used to preserve and store food. Those early pieces are valued by antique collectors today.

In addition to pottery, Pfaltzgraff markets high-quality stainless-steel flatware, glass beverageware, and decorative lighting items.

This is a finished product, in our very popular "Tea Rose" pattern, that's been through a second firing. One of the things that makes it so popular is its mat or dull finish. This is another feature of Pfaltzgraff products that a lot of our competitors aren't able to do as well. At this point the product goes through a final inspection and is ready to go to our distribution center for packaging and shipping to our consumers. ⑬

13

PHILLIPS
MUSHROOM FARMS, L.P.

Location	Phillips Mushroom Farms 1011 Kaolin Road Kennett Square, PA 19348 (610) 925-0520 www.phillipsmushroomfarms.com
Hours	No public tours available. Museum open daily, 10:00 a.m. to 6:00 p.m. Call (800) 243-8644 for information.
Tour Guide	Jim Angelucci General Manager

We're in Avondale, PA, overlooking Laurel Valley Farms, a commercial composter that makes compost for twelve mushroom farms in southern Chester County. The mushroom industry started in Kennett Square a hundred years ago. It is the original recycler. ①

1

With 260 employees and 750,000 square feet of production area, supplying over 45 million pounds of mushrooms annually, Phillips Mushroom Farms is the largest grower and marketer of specialty mushrooms in the country.

Mushroom compost is made by taking mulch hay, which is timothy, alfalfa, and clover unsuitable for feed, and combining it with horse manure from race tracks. The horse manure is mixed together with other nutrients such as cottonseed hulls, poultry manure, and corn cobs, combined into a mixture that is picked up by large machines, and mixed into a specific formulation that will eventually grow the mushroom crop. From the time the raw material is brought to the wharf until it's completed takes about 25 to 30 days. This material is combined on a set schedule to ensure that we have proper aeration in the substrate mixture. Temperatures in the organic matter are monitored on a daily basis to ensure that there is enough oxygen to allow the microbes to grow that will eventually convert the ammonia and nitrogen into protein that the mushroom can utilize. The compost is then taken from this facility to the mushroom farm, where it is placed into the rooms to be pasteurized and allow the conversion process to continue.

We're now at the mushroom farm, standing in front of one of Phillips' environmentally controlled growing rooms. Mushrooms are grown 365 days a year, in rooms where we control the environment. The compost that you saw earlier was delivered to this room at the beginning of this week. The compost temperature is generally about 140 degrees Fahrenheit. The temperature in the air is about 100 degrees. We allow enough oxygen to go into the room to ensure that we continue the growth of the microorganisms that will convert the nitrogen and protein into mushroom food. ②

Most of the mushrooms produced in the United States are of the white button variety. Last year about 800 million pounds were produced by 36 states.

On the fourth day we bring a portable steam boiler in, and we raise the temperature in the room to between 140 and 145 degrees. This temperature will be held for four hours. Research has shown that this time and temperature combination is sufficient to kill any of the pathogens that may be in the compost that would affect the mushroom crop. After the four-hour period, the room temperature will be brought down to about 100 degrees, and after a time the compost temperature will be brought to about 138 to 140 degrees. Once the pasteurization cycle is completed, we put filters into our ventilation system to ensure that anything that comes into the room is filtered out, and we provide an environment that will only grow the mushroom crop. This phase takes about 14 days to complete. This is where all of the protein is converted into food for the mushroom.

We're now in the next stage of mushroom production, which is called spawn run. Once the compost has completely converted, the pasteurization cycle is complete. Then we drop the temperature in the room down to about 70 degrees Fahrenheit. At that point the compost temperature comes down to about 75 to 80 degrees Fahrenheit, and that's when we actually seed or spawn the mushroom crop. Mushroom spawn is made by companies that specialize in it. It's done in a sterile process where cereal grain, wheat, rye, or millet is sterilized, it's inoculated with a culture of mushroom tissue, and the cultures are then placed in incubation rooms and allowed to grow. It takes 14 to 20 days for this mycelium to colonize the grain. And once that is completed, the mushroom spawn is placed in refrigerated rooms to ensure that the temperature won't increase to a level that would adversely affect the mushroom crop. When we as growers get the spawn, we throw it on the beds just like you would throw grass seed onto your lawn. ③

At that point we bring in a machine; we call it a spawning machine. It looks like a huge roto-tiller that is the width of the bed. It works its way up the bed by means of hydraulics and incorporates the mushroom spawn, the seed, with the compost to ensure that we get an even distribution from top to bottom, from side to side. Once the beds are fully spawned, we cover the surface with a layer of plastic. Plastic is used to help keep the moisture in the bed, and in addition it helps protect the surface from some of the pests that affect the mushroom crop.

Once we spawn the beds it takes 14 to 19 days for the mushroom mycelium to completely colonize the substrate.

In the spawn run room, the temperature is about 60 degrees Fahrenheit because we are trying to control the heat that's naturally generated by the mycelium. You can see this white, threadlike structure is now incorporating itself into the compost. This white substance you see is actually mushroom tissue in a vegetative state. ④ Mushrooms are obviously not like any green plants. They contain no chlorophyll, so we have to provide the food source. The food source is the mushroom compost. The other thing about mushrooms that differentiates them from green plants is that, like humans, they take in oxygen and give off carbon dioxide. In order to get this mushroom mycelium to grow through the compost, we keep the carbon dioxide level in the room high. Because carbon dioxide occurs naturally, it's just a matter of fixing the damper so that we don't bring fresh air into the room.

> Pennsylvania produces 47 percent of all the mushrooms grown in the United States.

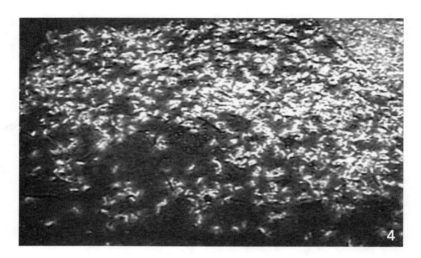

We next cover the mushroom surface with approximately two inches of Canadian peat moss that has been pasteurized to ensure that there are no pathogens in there that would affect the mushroom crop. And that surface, that casing layer, acts as a fruiting surface for the mushroom beds.

We're now in one of our rooms where the mushroom tissue has actually colonized the compost. As you can see by the side view, the mushroom tissue is completely colonized. ⑤ We put on a casing layer, which is the top two inches of pasteurized Canadian peat moss, and brought the room up to conditions that support

mushroom growth. We maintain the carbon dioxide at a high level to encourage the mycelium to move up through the casing layer vegetatively.

Once the mushroom tissue reaches the surface, we change the environment in the room. We do three things: we drop the temperature to about 60 degrees Fahrenheit; we drop the carbon dioxide level by closing the damper, bringing in fresh air; and we start to water the surface of the casing layer so that we can encourage this mushroom mycelium to knit together and form tiny fruit bodies. If you look very closely, you'll be able to see some of these pinheads, as we call them, which are very small, immature mushrooms that will eventually grow to the size that you see in your supermarket. From the time that we put the casing layer on the compost until we harvest the first mushroom is about 21 days. Once mushrooms start fruiting, they are harvested every day for the life of the crop. We're on a 13-week schedule, which means from the time we fill the house, until we fill it again, is 13 weeks. ⑥

Phillips Mushroom Farms is a third-generation, family-owned business. Family patriarch William Phillips began growing mushrooms in his hometown of Kennett Square in 1926.

Some of these mushrooms are much larger than others. The larger ones are the mushrooms that we allow to mature on the bed and become portabellas. If you look at the underside of a mushroom that is not mature, you can see that there is no break in the space between the stem and the cap. Those mushrooms have not reached their level of maturity. When we allow the mushroom to mature and become a portabella, this veil breaks. These gills that you see underneath the cap contain mushroom spores. ⑦ In the normal mushroom production this is not something that growers would like to have happen because once the mushroom cap opens, the microscopic spores are released. We then have the potential of inoculating some of the rooms that are in critical stages of production with viruses that would affect mushroom produc-

tion. If you recall, back in the pasteurization stage I mentioned that we put filters into the ventilation system to help stop that inoculation of rooms in critical stages of production.

So this is the way that portabella and crimini and white mushrooms are produced in Pennsylvania. From here the mushrooms are taken to the packing facility and cooled and packaged in the types of consumer boxes that you find in the supermarket.

This is a growing room for shiitakes. As you can see, the shiitake log looks like a loaf of bread. (8) It's actually held together by the white mycelium. It currently weighs about seven pounds, but as you can see, all of these shiitake mushrooms are fruiting on this log. Shiitake is a completely different species than a white mushroom. The growing parameters are different. It requires different levels of humidity, carbon dioxide, and refrigeration in order to get the mushroom to fruit. The other thing about growing shiitake logs is that, in order to get the moisture into these logs, they're put into plastic baskets and placed in tanks. The tanks are then filled with water, and the logs are submerged for a 24-hour period. By submerging them, that little bit of water pressure forces water into the log to promote the growth of the next crop. This is a first flush. Mushrooms grow in flushes. We will harvest these mushrooms, and about seven to ten days later the second flush of mushrooms will be produced.

The complete process of growing shiitake mushrooms now takes only three months. We took a process that generally took four to six years, and by controlling the environment, controlling humidity, controlling carbon dioxide, and controlling temperature, we produce shiitake mushrooms in a three-month period.

These are oyster mushrooms. (9) Inside these bags is pasteurized wheat straw. That's the substrate that we use to grow oyster mushrooms. We also add other nutri-

ents to it like cottonseed hulls, wheat bran, and millet grain. It takes about 15 days for the mushroom mycelium, that white mass that you saw before, to completely colonize this log. Then it takes three days after that for the mushrooms to start fruiting. Picking starts about four days after that. These mushrooms produce in flushes. Seven to ten days after the first flush is harvested, a second flush of mushrooms will be produced and harvested.

We're now inside our packing room. ⑩ Our portabella caps are placed on a machine that has been designed by Phillips to slice the mushrooms. The mushrooms are then put into tills, which in turn are fed into the packaging machine. The

mushrooms follow down a line, and the film is on a roll that has the label attached to it. This package goes through the machine where the film is laid over the surface of the till, is pulled together and heat-sealed, and comes off the other end. This is a type of package that you would see on the mushroom shelf in your local supermarket. ⑪

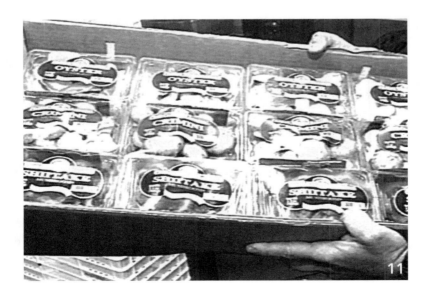

Phillips Mushroom Farms began experimenting with shiitake mushrooms in 1980. The company was the first successful commercial indoor shiitake grower in the United States.

Founder William Phillips' early experiments in using ice for temperature control during the summer months were a significant breakthrough for the mushroom industry, allowing mushrooms to be grown year-round.

Location	Reynoldsville Casket Company
	P.O. Box 68, Fifth Street Extension
	Reynoldsville, PA 15851
	(800) 441-8224
	www.reynoldsvillecasket.com
Hours	No public tours available.
	Factory tours are available to funeral directors and their staff by appointment.
Tour Guide	Rusty Meyers
	Plant Manager

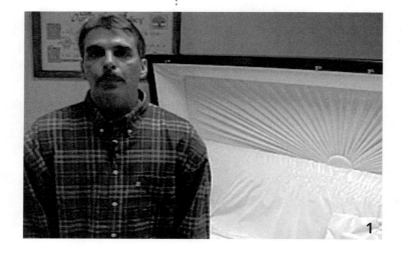

The history of Reynoldsville Casket goes back to 1912 when a company called Pennsylvania Burial moved from Brockville, PA, to this location. They manufactured caskets until the end of 1980, when they closed their doors. Our president, Wayne Jackson, and several local investors got together, reopened the doors, and started the Reynoldsville Casket Company. Today we employ more than 90 men and women who are devoted to manufacturing and distributing premium-quality caskets. We have a sales force that covers our customer base, which is the licensed funeral directors in licensed funeral homes. We have more than 600 accounts statewide and in bordering states. We also sell to distributors in areas as far away as Canada and Michigan. In 1998, we produced more than 14,500 caskets, of which 50 percent were custom-made. (1)

At the beginning of the production process, our welder takes two sides and two ends, puts them on his welding table, and welds the casket together, forming a solid base. ② This particular model is an 18-gauge protective. Reynoldsville Casket manufactures in 20-gauge, 18-gauge, 19-gauge, and 16-gauge steel. We also manufacture in metals such as bronze, copper, and stainless steel. It's very important that the welder get good penetration to ensure a tight weld. One individual welder in an eight-hour day can

weld anywhere from 40 to 55 caskets, depending upon the style. We have over 40 different base styles of caskets to choose from.

Next we'll see where we weld our precious metals. Our welder happens to be working on a solid copper casket. Once again, he has to make sure that his penetration welds are complete. Obviously, safety is very important to us at Reynoldsville Casket. Our welder is wearing a breathe-easy turbo welding helmet. The system makes sure that he's provided with enough oxygen. After the welders get done welding the base, they transfer the caskets up ahead of them to where the grinders work. ③

Once the lids have been welded, we have to grind the welds off to polish the steel. Once our grinder has the weld completely ground off and polished, he attaches the hinges to the back of the lid. They fit up underneath the lip, and this is what will attach the lid to the base of the casket. ④ It's very important that the grinders make sure they polish all of the grind marks. Once the grinder has finished grinding the casket, it is placed on the track where we install the bottom.

The company's 90 employees produce and sell 16,000 caskets per year.

This is our seam-welding position. ⑤ Inside the casket, the base has an inner ledge. Our welder is going to take the bottom, tack it to the ledge, take it over to the seam welder, and we'll have an automatic seamed, welded bottom. This particular process has been designed and engineered so that no water, air, or graveside substances can ever enter the casket. A seam welder is composed of 90 percent copper. Notice how the copper wheel will come down. It is actually fusing the bottom onto the sides and ends of the casket. Once our welder welds this final piece, he's completed the operation of the seam welder. He now takes the casket and tests it to make sure that we have an airtight seal. He does this by immersing the casket in water. By

using pressure, we force the casket down below the water level. Then we look inside to see if any water is entering the casket. If this happens, we know that the seam welder wasn't effective and the process has to be repeated.

The next position is where we take the lid and attach it to the base of the casket. We carry about 13 different tops that we can apply to the different base styles we have. This is the final step of the welding process, and now the casket will be sent into the prime shop, where we will prep it before we paint it. ⑥

This is the repair position. Our employee is looking for any imperfections in the steel, looking for any dents and scratches. ⑦ It's basically like auto body work, prepping the steel before we can treat it with paint. By rubbing his hands back and forth, he's feeling for any dent that might be in the casket. Once we've removed any scratches or dents, the casket is taken over to our de-greasing position, where it is

Caskets manufactured in the company's early years were made of wood purchased from nearby sawmills. Wood continued to be the primary material for casket construction until the late 1930s, when metal caskets became popular.

Originally, the company manufactured only the casket shells, which were then finished on the inside and outside by the funeral directors. During the 1918 influenza epidemic, funeral directors were unable to keep up with the demand for caskets, and began ordering them ready-fitted with interiors and hardware.

completely wiped down with a biodegradable cleaner, making sure we remove all of the dirt and grease left on it from the pressing operation.

Our next position is the priming position. The first part of this job is to prime the bottom of the casket. It is very important that we get good coats of primer. Our primer first takes a rag, wipes off any additional grease that might have been left over, and applies a light-colored gray, water-based primer. Then, using beeswax, he tacks off the casket. This is just to make sure that he picks up any loose dust particles that might be resting on the casket. Inside each casket as it comes up the line is a ticket that specifies the color, the style, the type of interior, and the type of decorative handles that the casket must have. Of the 14,000 that we produced last year, 50 percent were custom-made. Once the casket has been completely primed, it is put into the oven, where it is lightly baked. ⑧

When the casket comes out of the oven, the next phase is to lightly buff it. This particular casket had a brush finish applied to it, so it shows the natural beauty of the metal. ⑨ Our buffer is using a 320-grit sandpaper. Once again, she's lightly scuffing the primer. She's also using her hands while she's doing that, feeling for

any dents or any imperfections. This is the final process before the casket gets painted. It is extremely crucial. On this casket the lid is in two pieces. This is what is called a perfection-cut casket. Eighty-five percent of the caskets manufactured and sold in Pennsylvania are full cuts, where the lid is in one piece. Ninety-five percent of the caskets made in this country are what we call half couch—that is, the lid is cut in half, so just the top half can be opened.

In Reynoldsville Casket's state-of-the-art paint room, our painter reads the ticket to determine what color he needs to paint the casket. (10) We have over 40 different colors to choose from, 13 of which are in 55-gallon drums and run through stainless-steel lines. We use an electrostatic painting system. We have a positive-charged gun, we put a negative charge on the casket, and the material is attracted to it like a magnet. This cuts down on the volatile organic compounds that we're admitting into the atmosphere. It also gives us longer paint life. Each casket uses about a quart and a half of paint.

After the casket has been painted and shaded, we apply an acrylic lacquer over the top of it. This brings out the luster and shine in the casket. Again we take a beeswax rag and tack off the casket, eliminating any dust that might be on top. Just as with the painting system, the acrylic lacquer system uses an electrostatic gun. After the casket has been top-coated, it is placed into an infrared oven at roughly 290 degrees.

The next part of the operation is where the hardware is attached to the casket. (11) This is what the pallbearers will hold onto when the casket is being carried. This unit being worked on is called the "Peace Rose." It's an 18-gauge. We have over 300 different styles of hardware that we apply to our caskets. Hardware basically

comes in two styles: stationary and swing bar. This one happens to be stationary hardware. We take a ruler and measure where the lugs have to be put in place. Each one of those pieces has a set place where it needs to be.

In the sewing room, one of our workers is laying out some of our textile. This is a high grade of crepe that she's laying out onto the table. ⑫ We use a cutting table when we're doing mass cuttings. She'll probably have 30 to 40 interiors that she'll lay out, put a pattern down, and cut the individual pieces that are needed. Each interior is composed of 14 or 15 individual pieces that have to be processed.

Once the initial set is cut, the material is taken to the shearing position. Here a decorative design is put on by using thread on several of the pieces that are going to make up the interior. This particular machine looks like it has 12 or 13 needles. While these pieces are being sewn, on the other side of the room we have an employee working on blankets for the caskets. Every full-couch casket has a blanket that is roughly two yards long. ⑬

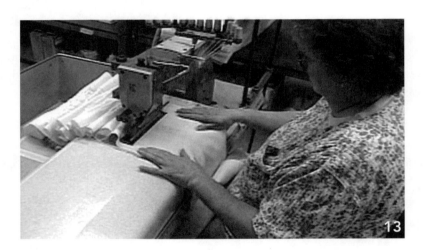

We call this the puffing position. ⑭ Here our employee is taking an embroidered panel and she's putting cardboard borders around the outside of it. This is the shearing that was put together in the sewing room. It has a nice decorative design to it.

The final step in our process is the popping of the panel and the closing. ⑮ Here a worker is taking the panel that was just made, and she's going to fit it inside the lid of the casket. While she's putting the panel in, we have another person on the other side of the room who is closing the casket down, checking once again to make sure the lock is completely adequate and that it seals properly. She'll look for any scratches, any defects that might have gotten past all of our quality checkpoints.

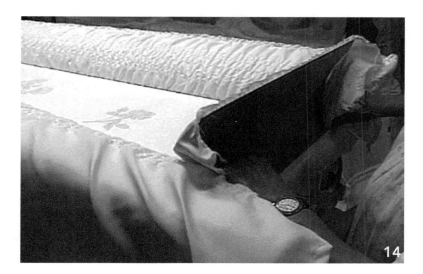

One of the final things that she'll do is buff out the top of that lid once again to ensure a nice shine.

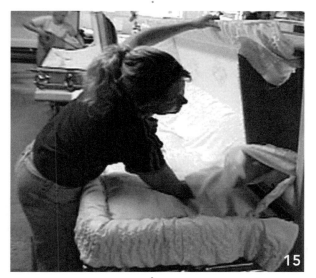

We ship out more than 60 caskets a day, but this business is very seasonal. Summer months are always the slow time of the year. When winter comes, things pick up a bit, mainly due to influenza and colds. We offer a complete line of caskets to funeral directors. We offer steel, copper, bronze, and stainless-steel models. We also make caskets in woods. We sell cloth-covered, cardboard, and fiberglass caskets. We have 190 individual units on our price list. Of the 14,000 that we manufactured last year, we made 2,000 different types. That is quite hard to do, but we have confidence in our work. We feel that we make a quality product. Obviously, it's made possible by the quality people that we have here.⃝16

Signature Door

Location	Signature Door Company 401 Juniata Street Altoona, PA 16602 (800) 741-2265 www.signaturedoor.com
Hours	No public tours available.
Tour Guide	Dennis Nixon, Jr. Vice President and CEO

Signature Door is located in Altoona, PA, and we're a manufacturer of oak entryways. Today we're going to take you on a tour of our operation, and show you the various processes that take place in a typical day here. Some of those processes will involve manufacturing of the door itself and the making of the glass panels. You will see us roll-forming our own brass, and you'll see our latest projects here, working with polyester resin that has a great resistance. We're going to demonstrate for you today that you can literally throw a baseball at a piece of glass and not worry about it breaking. That is also very good when it comes to security. So with that in mind, let's move forward and we'll start the tour. ①

A lot of times manufacturers will make a door out of a solid piece of wood. We do

too, but there's one difference. Ours is a piece of engineered wood. We take the solid oak and resaw it, then the grain is reversed and it's glued back together. Then on the top and the bottom we put a quarter-inch slice of oak and glue it all together. This takes the stresses out of the wood. That piece of wood will stay as straight as an arrow. You don't have to worry about it drying out and pulling, twisting, and bowing. So we feel it's a superior door. It costs us more to do this, but we save money in the long run, because our doors only go one way—out to the customer.

Now we're going to show you the veneering operation. We're doing laminating for elliptical transoms and round tops. We use a small glue machine that spreads the glue onto the veneers. As the veneers run across the rollers, a predetermined amount of glue is put on the bottom side of each piece. ②

The pieces of veneer are then stacked, and we continue to stack them until we get the desired thickness. Sometimes we may have to glue as many as 20 pieces, depending on the profile we're doing. If it's a very tight bend, we will use a sixteenth-of-an-inch veneer. So just to get an inch thickness, you need to glue 16 pieces of that veneer together. ③

Now we're going to take this veneer that's glued together and put it in the clamp. The clamp table has adjustable fingers that allow us to bend the veneer into any shape we desire. We put a band of shrink-wrap around each end to keep the

pieces from sliding all over. At this stage they're pretty slippery. The first thing we do is to clamp the center. Next we attach a heat band that will help set the glue for us. These are air clamps that will be attached from the center out. After our worker puts the last clamp on, he can go into the shop and perform another duty, because this is going to take about 30 minutes to cure. ④

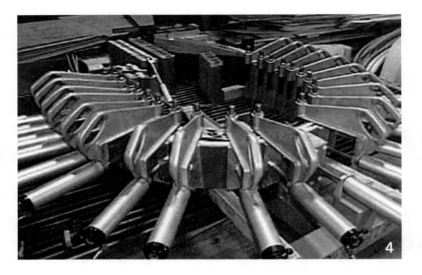

With sales exceeding $5 million per year, Signature Door markets its doors from coast to coast through independent sales representatives. It targets the small lumber yards, as its goal is to help smaller businesses compete with the mass merchants.

When the piece is cured, the clamps can be taken off, and what we'll get is a part that looks just like this. ⑤ The piece shown here has two oak bands and three aspen bands.

To test the endurance and breaking point of its doors, the company exposed a door to positive and negative pressures equal to an 800 mph wind velocity. Although an oak portion of the door failed at 800 mph, the door remained operational.

Now we'll see the sidelight put together. You might notice that the dowels have a spiral on them. That allows an area for the glue, and gives you a much stronger hold. If that were just a solid dowel, when you drove the dowel into the hole, most of the glue would be pushed right out. But the spiral allows the glue to stay in and put a good hold on the door. You notice the doors we make here at Signature Door have a lot of handwork in them. It's not a high-production operation. ⑥

When we take the clamps and draw the door up, you'll see the glue squeezing out, and that assures us that we have enough in there. We'd rather have too much than not enough. We will draw the clamps up and set the door aside, and let it acclimate for no less than 24 hours. We just pressed a lot of glue into that wood, and there's a lot of moisture in it. And if we were to take the clamps off an hour from now and sand it, the glued area would shrink down, and then it would not be level. We want to dissipate the moisture, and then we will sand the door evenly. ⑦

On the next page you see some doors ready to sand. We'll run them through our wide-belt sander. We start out with 60-grit, step up to 100, and then 150 for the final run. We first set the height. We normally take about three sixty-fourths of an inch off each side. Each door is run through the sander a minimum of four times. This sanding process assures us that the surface of the door is level. After the first round of side one, we will flip the door over and run it through again. Then we will put on the 150-grit belt and run it through two more times. ⑧

At the assembly table, we install the frames to hold the glass and the panels in the door. At this point we will install the glass insert. We bed our panels and glass in silicone, which is not only a sealant, but a glue as well, and it allows the door parts to move a little. You have a better chance for problems if you glue the panel in tightly. Glass does not expand and contract the same as wood, so you have to use something with some give to it. That's why we have chosen silicone. The bead of silicone seals the door, but will also hold the glass. After that we shoot an inch-and-a-quarter brad into the molding to hold it in place. Really, all that does is hold the molding in place until the silicone sets, because once that silicone sets, it just doesn't come out. ⑨

The company was founded in 1989 by Dennis Nixon and Bernd Lewkowitz, who had a goal of manufacturing a door in the United States that could compete with doors that were being imported from other countries.

Our newest glass is resin glass. And what I'd like to do is take a minute and show you how well this glass resists breaking. I'm going to stand this door up and have an employee take a baseball and whale it at this piece of glass while I'm standing behind it. ⑩ All right, I'm ready. Here's your chance to let the boss have it. Don't see any damage, do you? Wouldn't everybody love to have one of those on their front door?

What Dave is going to demonstrate here is our new break-resistant and high-security glass. We're going to show you how much that glass can slow a man down. ⑪ When Dave hits that glass, it's not going anywhere. After taking a crowbar to it, he still has to work his way through it. Let's show you how we make that glass.

Here is where we make the protector glass. First we mix the resin, then we pour the resin between two pieces of tempered glass. We have 30 thousandths of an inch of space between those two pieces of glass. After we fill that cavity, we will lay that sheet level and let it cure for about 24 hours. ⑫ If we then tilt the table, the resins flow forward, and at each corner we have a little opening that allows the air to escape. When the resin reaches that point, we will seal that opening. A little bit of sealant bonds the two pieces of glass together, and that's what keeps the unit intact when you beat on it with a crowbar.

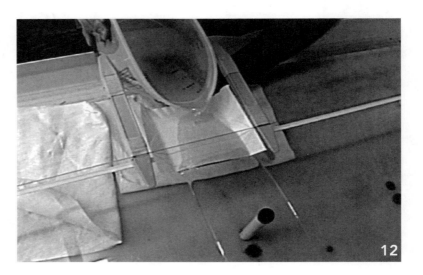

When the business opened, it had one employee, Dennis Nixon. Within the first year, the staff grew to seven. Today the company employs 74 people and has a facility of 36,500 square feet.

Now we're going to show you how we cut the glass. When we started out, we didn't have this computerized glasscutter. We used to hand-cut with Masonite templates that we made in-house. But about three years ago we graduated to this glasscutter, which is computer-controlled. ⑬ There's a carbide wheel that runs across the glass and fractures the surface. So when we say glass cutting, we really mean glass scoring. Prior to purchasing this machine, we had three people cutting glass full time, all day long. Since we purchased the machine, we've had one person who just breaks or snaps out the pieces. As he's snapping out one sheet, the cutter is scoring another sheet.

This machine is very accurate. You can cut a hundred pieces and stack them up, and they're right on the money. It took me a few years to find a machine that

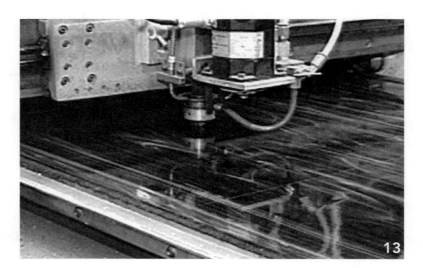

would cut as accurately as we needed. It's nice to know that this machine is made in Pennsylvania.

Here we are at the assembly table. We saw the glass being cut; the tails were then ground off, the bevels were checked, and now we are putting it together. ⑭ If you know how to put a puzzle together, you may have a job at Signature Door. After this panel is assembled, it will be put on the table, and people who do the soldering will pick it up. Usually we'll have an individual put the same window together, especially if we have an order for 25 or 50. The same person will put all those units together.

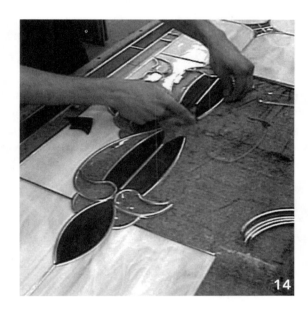

Next we move to the solder station. This is what holds the unit together. The solderer dips the tip of the solder into the flux, touches the tip of the solder down to the brass so that the flux will run, and brings the heat gun down to melt the solder. It's very labor-intensive. A typical panel needs about five person-hours from start to finish, including the cutting of the glass, the cutting of the brass, the rolling, and the cleaning. After a unit is soldered, we take it into what we call the "clean room" and flush it out with water. The reason we do that is to get rid of all the fluxes left there. If we leave a flux, a couple years down the road it will corrode the brass, so we want to make sure it's all washed out. ⑮

After washing, the panel is put on the belt. That belt is moving, but very slowly. It's about a 20-minute ride through a heat tunnel from one end to the other. What we're doing here is chasing all of the moisture out of the channel. We need to bring

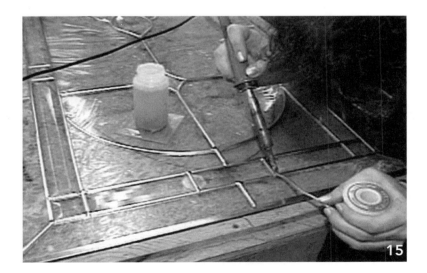

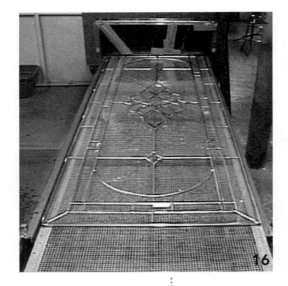

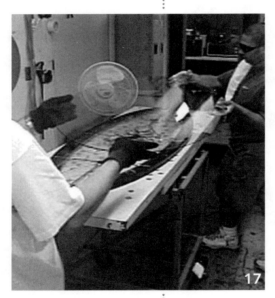

the panel up to about 240 degrees, but you have to bring it up slowly or you'll break the glass. So that's the purpose of the long tunnel. (16)

The units are pretty toasty coming out of the tunnel. They go into a room where we have a controlled environment to keep the dust and the dirt down. At that point the windows look fairly clean, but we do a final inspection where we work with Q-tips, razor blades, whatever it takes to get the window as clean as a human can get it. Because after this we insulate it, and we can never get back in to touch it up. So it's critical that it be as clean as possible.

Now we'll move forward and show you where we insulate these panels. Almost everything we insulate here at Signature Door is done using what we call the warm-edge technology. If you look closely, there is a corrugated metal strip inside of that butyl layer. That gives it support and acts as a moisture barrier. Now we take a clean piece of glass and lay it on top, creating a sandwich. (17) Our decorative panels are sandwiched between two pieces of safety glass. Then it goes on the press, and the heat lamps come on and give it intense heat. We can bring that glass to within two or three thousandths of an inch of where we want it. So the tolerances are very close.

What we're looking at now is a prehung door unit we've just finished up. (18) After the door is hung, it's rolled into the crating area and put on a crate in an A-frame. Then we'll put on a shrink-wrapper to protect it and hold everything together. We will ship a prehung unit anywhere in the country this way. Not only just a door, but a door with two sidelights, a door with a transom, you name it. The shrink-wrap also allows our customer to inspect it when it arrives on the truck, so that he does not have to open the crate. He can look right through the clear wrap and verify that his door arrived in good condition.

Location	Story & Clark Pianos
	269 Quaker Drive
	Seneca, PA 16346
	(814) 676-6683
	www.storyandclark.com
Hours	Public tours available by appointment.
Tour Guide	John Omiatek
	Director of Technical Services

Hello and welcome to Story & Clark Piano Company. This company started here in Seneca, PA, in 1986. We were making one player piano a day. We got a little bit larger and continued that production through the end of the 1980s. In 1996, we started building grand pianos at this location.

Our piano-making begins with the back assembly. When you look at the back of the piano, this is what you're going to see. ① We call them the back posts. This

1

is a post-and-filler block design, and this is the first step in building the piano. This is all hard Pennsylvania maple from right around here, and we're proud of that fact.

The next step is to install the soundboard and the pin block. These are very important parts of the piano. We call the soundboard the heart of the piano, and the pin block is going to hold all of the tuning pins.

What we're seeing here is our operator cleaning up the glue joint on the treble bridge of the piano that he has just fitted onto the soundboard. Just so you know what we're looking at, this is the soundboard of the piano already installed. On the left is the pin block, a very special piece of the piano. It's made of hard rock maple, 90 percent cross-laminated for strength. When we put the tuning pins into this piano, we're going to be drilling 225 holes in the pin block and installing all the pins. It's very important that this piece maintain its structural integrity over the years because that's what keeps your piano in tune. Our operator is finishing the treble bridge installation. The next step will be to install the bass bridge. Then this assembly will be ready to go up front, where we will set the plate on this piano. ②

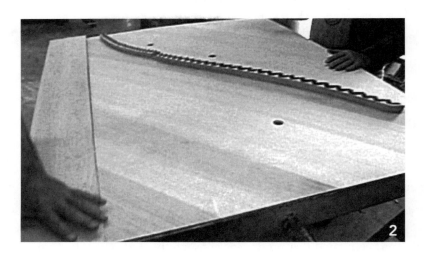

This is the assembly. After the treble bridge and the bass bridge are installed, the next step is to install the cast-iron piano plate. Our operator here is shimming the plate. ③ It's quite a precise operation for an assembly this large and this heavy. It's

amazing how precise we have to be when we set this. What we do is have the string go up over the bridge and back down the other side, somewhat like you would see on a guitar or a violin. In a piano, even with an assembly this large, we have about a 50,000th of an inch to work with over the entire length of this treble bridge, which is quite precise. That's why we'll see our operator here doing so many different measurements using some specialized tools and a lot of straight edges. If our operator makes a mistake, we have a factory second, and we don't want that to happen very often. This is a 164-pound plate for a 42-inch console piano. This is quite a massive back assembly. We've built about 7,500 of these assemblies here at this plant since 1990.

Our next station is piano-stringing. The treble wires go on first, and the bass set goes across in a different direction. What you see is note number 88 on the piano, the shortest string. ④ The speaking length of that string is somewhere around $2\frac{1}{4}$ inches. That's when you're hearing the very high pitch of the piano. You can see that the wires are different sizes as we go down into the lower notes. We will continue installing the treble wires the whole way down the bridge. Then we'll add the bass strings, which we'll string over the other way. That allows us to have longer piano strings in a shorter piano.

This is our finish-sanding table. Every piece of lumber that comes through this wood shop is inspected and sanded here. This one is probably almost ready for the stain. The people here have to sand every little part of this very finely to make it finish nicely. ⑤

Although we have a few machines, almost every procedure here is done by hand. So the piano is actually hand-built. No one has come up with a better way to make a piano in the last 100 years.

This is our staining shop. Here we're using cherry stain, which is hand-applied and brushed by our operators. ⑥ Most of the stains that we use are hand-wipe and wipe-off stains. But some of them require special brushing techniques to make the stain come out evenly and to cover the wood nicely. This board is going to be part of a $4,000 or $5,000 piano, so it's very important that it look just right. Along with staining, another part of the operation here at this station is to color-match or tone all of the parts. What we're doing is trying to make all the different hardwoods and veneers come out to the exact same shade of cherry, in this case.

At this point the piano is starting to look like a piano, and our operator is getting ready to locate the piano action. When he is finished with that action, tightening screws and doing a lot of small procedures, he will be putting it into the piano. He'll

check every screw in the action to make sure it's tight. This is a Baldwin-made part. We don't make enough pianos here to efficiently make our own piano actions, and you can get a little bit of an idea of how complex a piano action is. If one flange is loose, we might change a pin from a 50,000th to a 51,000th of an inch. So it's a very precise operation, and of course it has to be done for all 88 notes. ⑦

The next step will be to prepare our hammers for the piano. Here we have a full set of hammers that is being prepped for installation. We're going to do some things to the hammers, like sand them off smooth and clean up any dead felt. The hardness of these hammers is important in achieving the tone we are trying to get from the piano. ⑧

At our next station, we will start the damper installation and regulation. Our operator has installed the set of dampers. You can see all the felt and wood blocks that quiet the string when you release the pedal or release the key. ⑨ This is a very critical part of the operation. What our operator is doing is trying to set every damper to lift off the string at exactly the same time. That's very important to the way the piano plays and feels. And it's quite a tedious job. It takes a very good eye to be able to see what we call a tiny wink of movement in that damper. All of the adjustments are done to that wire that you see our operator bending. This is one of those operations that take months to learn how to do well.

On the following page you see our operator putting the finishing touches on this key set. It has already been installed and leveled. She's adjusting the keys or regulating them to the piano action. The keys are set to within five to seven thousandths of an inch of each other. It makes the piano play uniformly and feel good. When she's finished at this station, the piano will go on for its final tuning and the cabinet-finishing. ⑩

This station is the first step in building our grand piano. We call this part the inner rim assembly. ⑪ It's all built from hard maple and some laminates on the rim itself. What we're doing here is gluing the parts together and keeping them in this press until dry. When that's done it is ready to go on to the next station, where we'll install the soundboard. This one here is a high-grade Eastern white spruce soundboard, and we've got it clamped and already crowned. So what we're doing in this stage is attaching it to the inner rim of the piano. This is the beginning of a pretty nice grand piano.

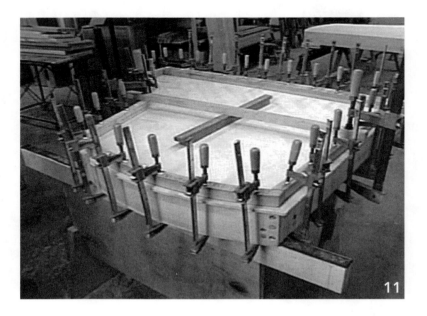

The next step, after the soundboard is glued and installed, is the fitting of the bridges to the piano. This is one of those operations that take quite a long time.

What we're doing is hand-shaving this bridge to fit the shape of our crowned soundboard. Our soundboard is in the piano at a crown or a radius that's similar to about a 70-foot circle, and what we're doing is hand-fitting this bridge to exactly match that curvature. Once that's all finished, our operator will glue the bridge to the soundboard. ⑫

Our operator is working here on leveling this grand key set. It's somewhat similar to what we saw in the upright piano line, although it's a little more complicated. She's placing different-colored thicknesses of "punchings" under the center of each key, and that dictates the height of the front of the key. ⑬

The company's original name was Classic Player Piano. The company produced one piano with eight employees. Still at the same location, the production facility has grown from the original 7,000 square feet to the current 55,000 square feet.

When she's finished with that, she's also going to be setting the dip. That is what we call how far each key travels to the bottom, so the piano plays uniformly and feels good.

At this point we are very close to having this piano finished. Here our operator is doing the final touch-up on a set of dampers, which travel up and down in a grand piano, as opposed to what we saw in the vertical piano line. It takes eight to ten hours to install a set of dampers, so they're quite precise. She is regulating or adjusting them by bending the metal wire that holds the damper. (14) And of course, she's going to set them so they fall very freely and don't make noise. It makes the piano feel and play well. When she finishes with this step, she'll be ready to slide the piano action and key set, which are finished on the table, into the piano, and do some of the final regulation steps before this piano goes to the spray shop. When it leaves this room, this piano will be ready to play.

Classic Player Piano purchased the well-known Story & Clark Piano Company in 1990, and began production of console and studio pianos using Story & Clark scale designs.

Story & Clark also manufactures nickelodeons, which incorporate a piano, twelve percussion instruments, and "Pianomation" automation. The percussion instruments include castanets, triangle, finger cymbals, glockenspiel, wood block, snare drum, bass drum, tambourine, and cow bell.

This piano action and key set is ready to install on that piano. And you can see the complexities of a grand piano action. It's pretty amazing compared to what we just saw in the upright pianos. This is a Czech-made action, and the key set is hand-made in Portland, OR. What we're doing here is mating the two, hand-fitting the hammers, doing all the key work and the dampers, and we figure about 50 hours per piano for all of the tech work involved. (15)

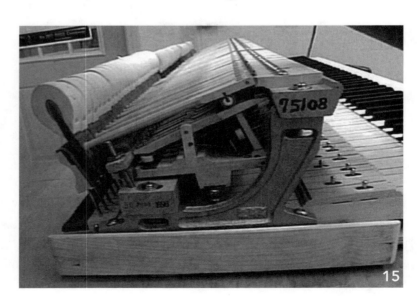

After our operator finishes with her damper set and reinstalls the action, which has been out of the piano quite a number of times, she'll do a lot of final adjustments and then we're ready to do the final tuning on this piano.

This is the grand piano that we had always wanted to build here. This is probably piano number 65, and it's quite a nice instrument. ⑯

Straub

SINCE 1872
BREWERY INC.

Location	Straub Brewery 303 Sorg Street St. Marys, PA 15857 (814) 834-2875 www.straubbeer.com
Hours	Public tours available Monday through Friday, 9:00 a.m. to 12:00 noon. No children under 12 admitted. Gift shop open Monday through Friday, 9:00 a.m. to 5:00 p.m.; Saturday, 9:00 a.m. to 1:00 p.m.
Tour Guide	Thomas Straub Brewmaster, Plant Manager, and Vice President

Hello, my name is Thomas Straub. I'd like to welcome you to Straub Brewery. The brewery was founded in 1872 by my great-grandfather, who came over from Germany. Straub Brewery is a family-owned brewery, and it has been in the family ever since its inception. ①

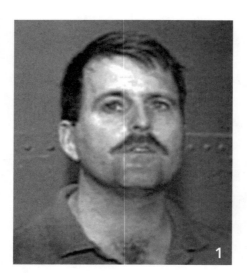

We are starting our tour in the mill room, where we start the production of beer.

What we have here is a mill. ② The mill grinds or crushes the malted barley, which is one of the primary ingredients in making beer, before it goes into our mash tub, which we will see a little later. A lot of people think a mill grinds the malted barley into flour. But this mill rips the grain apart. It keeps the husks pretty much intact, because the husks will serve

as a primary filter medium in our mash tub. The mill crushes the inside part, which is the starchy part, and it dissolves and becomes the extract of the beer we will make.

The process of making beer actually begins before the malted barley gets to us here at the brewery, and that step is the malting process. That is where maltsters take selected barley and they malt it by germinating the grain. Germination of the grain modifies the starches and activates the natural enzymes in the malted barley, which will convert the starches to fermentable sugars in our mash tub.

During the brewing process our primary ingredient is water. The water we use here at the brewery is from the St. Marys Water Company. It is a spring-fed reservoir, but the water is chlorinated. Before we use that water for brewing, we put it through our own filters. Our filters consist of anthracite, sand, gravel, and activated carbon. So we neutralize, or take out, the chemicals that the water company puts into the water. We like to think that we have an excellent water source here, probably one of the better water sources in the country.

Here in these jars are three of the four primary ingredients of beer. ③ The first jar contains cornflakes, which are similar to what you would eat in the morning, except that they are a little smaller, and they are not roasted or sugar-coated. The second jar contains a sample of malted barley, and the barley is in this form when we

The company now employs 40 people and occupies a 40,000-square-foot plant, where it has been located for 129 years.

In 2000, Straub Brewery produced 36,000 barrels of beer. In the beer industry, 31 gallons equals one barrel. Of that production, 85 percent was Straub Beer and 15 percent was Straub Light.

The company can bottle up to 128 bottles per minute of nonreturnables and 100 bottles per minute of returnables.

get it. As I mentioned earlier, we will crush the malted barley to free the starches, which will eventually become the extract, which is the main component of the beer.

In the third jar we've got hops. This is what hops look like when they are harvested. Years ago all breweries used hops in this form, but it was somewhat unsanitary and hard to get a standardized product. So now the hops companies take the raw product, concentrate it, and produce an extract. These canned hops allow the brewer to have a standardized product. Years ago we would get a truckload of hops. In the first week the hops would be different than they would be six months later. It was tough to get a consistent product. So with modern technology we now purchase a hops extract.

This is our brew kettle. This is where we boil the hot wort after we draw the extract from the grain, and where starches are converted to sugars by natural enzymes present in the malted barley. We draw the extract off, it flows to the kettle, and we fill the brew kettle. As we do so, we add hops. ④

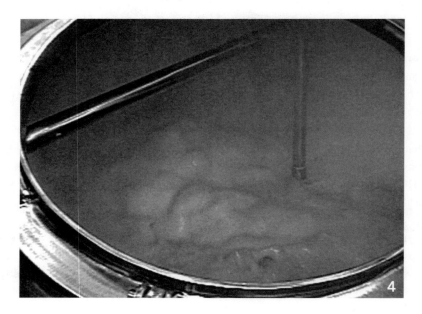

After the kettle is filled, we boil it for approximately two hours. At this point, the hot wort will be pumped up to our hot wort tank. Then from the hot wort tank it will be pulled down through a heat exchanger and cooled, and yeast will be added. The kettle boil is quite important for a number of reasons. It helps coagulate proteins that are present in the wort. It also thoroughly mixes the ingredients. You will see the violent rolling of the kettle. There is actually a percolator in the kettle, similar to what you would see in an old coffee pot. It superheats the wort, and sends the hot wort up through the barrel percolator, giving us a violent action in there. If we didn't have the violent action, we would have scorching on the bottom, and we wouldn't have adequate mixing. ⑤

After the two-hour kettle boil has taken place, we pump the hot wort mixture up to our hot wort tank, where the proteins that coagulated during the boil will settle out. So at this point in the process, the hot wort is further clarified before we cool the wort and add the yeast. The hot wort tank is a stainless-steel tank. It's a whirlpool-type tank, where the hot wort is pumped from the kettle. The entire con-

tents of the kettle, which is approximately 145 barrels, is pumped up to the wort tank in a matter of about 25 to 30 minutes. And that's a pretty fast pumping rate.

Basically, a hot wort tank is a big settling tank. The hot wort will be drawn through our heat exchanger, where we will pull the hot wort from 190 degrees Fahrenheit down to about 50 degrees Fahrenheit. After cooling, we add air to the mixture and inject yeast. Now the heat exchanger not only cools the wort, but it preheats water. That preheated water, after it leaves the heat exchanger, will fill another tank. So during the process of cooling the hot wort from today's brew, we will preheat water for tomorrow's brew.

The cooling room is where we cool the hot wort that we produced in our brew house. This is the step that the hot wort takes before it goes into fermenting. Let's stop and review what hot wort is. In our brew house we mix the ingredients of water, malted barley, and cornflakes. All of these ingredients are mixed together in our mash tub, where natural enzymes present in the malted barley convert the starches into fermentable sugars. We draw off that clarified extract from the mash tub and transfer it to the kettle. We then boil the mixture. At this point in the process, the mixture is called wort or hot wort. The hot wort is pumped from the kettle up to our hot wort tank. Then from our hot wort tank we draw that hot mixture down through a pump and into our heat exchanger. We pull the hot wort from approximately 190 degrees Fahrenheit down to approximately 50 degrees Fahrenheit.

After cooling has taken place, the cooled wort leaves the heat exchanger, and we add yeast to the mixture. Now the mixture is what we call green beer, and it goes to one of our fermenting tanks.

We are now in our main cellar here at the brewery. ⑥ Our main cellar is where we have

storage tanks and one of our fermenting rooms. Our fermentation takes seven days. At that point the beer still has yeast in it, although fermenting is completed. The beer is dropped from the fermenting tanks down through a cooler, where we chill it to 32 degrees. We hold it in our storage tanks for approximately a week, then it goes through primary filtering, secondary filtering, and on into our finish tank.

The process shown here is called racking, or filling the kegs. ⑦ This is one of our two packaging lines. This particular machine is a three-arm racker. We've got three kegs that are being filled at once. Beer is pumped from a finish tank downstairs into the reservoir tank.

Once the keg is filled, our keg-filler will pick up a wooden bung and he'll hammer the bung into the keg. Now, he's only got about three seconds to hammer the bung into the keg. If he misses it, he'll have a fountain of beer and a keg that will have to be rewashed, and it won't be able to be sold. ⑧

Our beer takes about three weeks from the day it's brewed to the day it's packaged and ready for the consumer.

Born in the village of Felldorf, Germany, in 1850, founder Peter Straub came to the United States in 1869, at the age of 19.

We buy our bottles brand-new. But in case of any dust in transit, we wash them as a precautionary measure. Here you can see our bottle-rinser. You'll notice that the bottles are being twisted and drained and then set right side up again as they come out the other side. ⑨

After the bottles are filled and capped, they are rinsed. At this point, they go through our bottle pasteurizer, and the bottles are gradually heated from 38 degrees Fahrenheit up to room temperature. ⑩

The last stop on our tour is the "Eternal Tap," which demonstrates Straub Brewery's hospitality. The tap is open to all of our visitors and guests, as long as they're at least 21 years of age, of course. ⑪

> The Straub Brewery was born when Peter Straub purchased the Benzinger Spring Brewery from his father-in-law, Francis Xavier Sorg.

Location	Sunline Coach Company
	245 South Muddy Creek Road
	Denver, PA 17517
	(888) 478-6546
	www.sunlinerv.com
Hours	Public tours available by appointment,
	Monday through Friday, 8:30 a.m., 10:30 a.m.,
	1:30 p.m., and 3:00 p.m.
Tour Guide	Mel Weiler
	Plant Manager

Hi, my name is Mel Weiler, plant manager here at Sunline Coach. We're about to take a tour of the production assembly line. We'll be right in there seeing how we put our trailers together. ①

The thing we start with is a frame. The frames are made off-site. The frame you see on the next page is sitting upside down. This is when we add the hitch, put the axles on, run the brake wires, and attach other equipment to the underside of the frame. ②

As we build the floor section of the trailer, we start with a wooden frame, and lay a one-piece trans-board flooring over it. You can see the bottom side of the floor. ③ It already has the insulation installed. Next we'll fasten the holding tanks that will go underneath the floor.

Those are the tanks that will hold the waste water and the septic water. They are mounted underneath the floor. At this point, when the floor is lying upside down, we will also install the wheel wells. After that we take the whole floor, with the tanks already mounted, and mount it onto the frame.

The next thing that needs to be done is to put in the appliances like the furnace, the heat ducts, and the freshwater tank. And every trailer has its own water heater.

Here one of our workers is building the door-side sidewall. ④ He has a pattern on the table so he knows where each piece of wood has to go. He's working at this point on the bottom of the sidewall. He usually does 10 or 20 of these walls that are very similar, one after the other. Once he sets the wood in place, he staples it all together.

He's using an air staple gun, which has a trigger and a safety. After he fastens everything together, he'll glue the panel on top, and then he'll rout out the windows and doors.

This is the next step in building the sidewalls. (5) The panel being worked on comes in four-by-eight sheets. We have a pattern that we lay that panel on, then we rout out the window openings, and rout out the extra wood on the front and back ends. Our worker is using an electric router, and cutting off the excess panel parts. He will contour the front end according to the design, then he'll round all of the openings that go inside, like a window or a door. The sidewall is already framed out, as you saw earlier, and when he uses the router, he just follows the shape of the frame inside and cuts the panel out. Here he's cutting a window opening.

Sunline Coach was incorporated in 1968, and moved to its present location the following year. The Denver, PA, facility encompasses 73,000 square feet.

This is a finished sidewall. The framework is done, the paneling is attached, and everything is glued and stapled and fastened together. You're looking at a sidewall from the inside. The window openings are cut out, the luggage door is cut out, and you can see where the furnace will come through the wall. (6) At this point the

In 1993, the company purchased the former Shasta plant in Leola, PA. That facility enabled Sunline to build longer travel trailers and slide-out rooms.

back doesn't have a finished panel, because that will be the bathroom area, where we will install a tub surround. So right now that's just a raw panel. The glue will hold better to the raw panel when we glue in our tub surround.

The other thing that happens in this area is a lot of the electrical wiring. If you look on the side, you can see that the wiring is being run through the sidewall. Those are the wires for the interior lights, for the furnace, for the thermostat, and for the TV cable. The next step will be to put the insulation on over top of the wires. ⑦

As we go inside, you can see that the appliances are being installed. The refrigerator and the range hood will be put in, and the 12-volt lights will be put up. Right here our worker is putting in the stereo. ⑧ Most of our units come with a stereo. This particular unit has ducted air-conditioning, so the vents for that are in the ceiling.

Now we're starting to put on the exterior skin. Most of our units are made with aluminum sides, fronts, and backs, and with a rubber roof. At this point they're getting ready to put the side aluminum on, and then they'll put on the roof. Most of the work is done not with machines but with a lot of hand labor. In this building we have approximately 90 production workers, and they each have their part to do. ⑨

Today, Sunline produces slide-out models up to 36 feet long, and more towable trailer models in the 19-to-30-foot range than any other manufacturer.

Here our worker has his metal laid out. ⑩   He's using aluminum, and he's cutting it to size. The aluminum comes as one piece for the whole side. Again it's fastened with staple guns. He's cut out all of the openings for the lights, for the windows, and for any of the appliances that have to be vented to the outside. Each piece has an S-lock that locks into the piece above it. He starts at the top and works to the bottom. He slides a piece into the S-lock and attaches it underneath, and the next piece will come up and cover up the staples where he fastened it.

As we look along this edge, the metal on the side comes up and wraps over it. There's a putty sealer added to the edge and another putty sealer put in on top. Then we have a corner molding that goes on top of that, so we have a double seal on the corner. After we put the corner molding on, we'll run screws right through it. Then we take this plastic insert and squeeze it in there. It covers up all of the screws, so you get a nice-looking finish. ⑪

If you look on this side you can see that we've put in the windows and installed the molding that covers the screws. We have also installed the outside vent for the range hood, the vent for the refrigerator, the flue for the water tank, the outside receptacle, and the water tank drain. We've also added the interior trim work like the mirror, the paper towel holder, a grab handle, and the curtains. Then everything gets cleaned up. ⑫

At this point the trailer is pretty well finished and ready to head out the door. We've seen it go from just the frame to having everything cut, installed, and cleaned up. It's now ready for shipment down the road to our dealer and from there to go camping. ⑬

Location	Utz Quality Foods
	900 High Street
	Hanover, PA 17331
	(800) 367-7629
	www.utzsnacks.com
Hours	Public tours available Monday through Thursday, 7:30 a.m. to 4:30 p.m. Groups of 12 or more should call in advance.
Tour Guide	Gary Laabs
	Vice President of Human Resources

Today we're going to tour the High Street facility of Utz Quality Foods, where we make our potato chips and tortilla chips. Utz Quality Foods was started in 1921 by Bill and Salie Utz. Salie would make chips in a room behind their house, and Bill would sell them door-to-door in Hanover. Soon the popularity of those chips grew, and Bill started to market them at carnivals, fire company fairs, and ultimately moved to farmers' markets in the Baltimore area. Today Utz is still owned by the same family. Mike Rice, who is chairman and CEO, is the grandson of Bill and Salie Utz. Please come with me now for a tour of Utz Quality Foods. (1)

We receive potatoes from storage in various locations throughout the United States. Primarily, we receive potatoes from Michigan and New York state. Additionally, we have potatoes in our own storage that we use throughout the winter. On an average production day, we'll go through about 600,000 pounds of potatoes. The potatoes that you see here are horticulturally designed to make good potato chips.

1

These potatoes would not be good as baking potatoes, but they are excellent for making chips. ②

In the spring of the year, we will get potatoes from Florida, and then we'll follow the harvest up the East Coast. When we get into August and September, we'll start putting potatoes into storage. Those will come from the northern tier of states, including North Dakota, Michigan, Wisconsin, New York, and Pennsylvania. We do occasionally get potatoes from Idaho, but as I mentioned earlier, our potatoes are specifically for making potato chips, and most of the potatoes grown in Idaho are for baking and kitchen use.

When potatoes come in on the conveyor, the first thing that happens is they go through a grader. The machine has a large screen in it. The size of the holes in that screen allows the smaller potatoes to fall through. That way we are able to sort the potatoes into specific sizes. Many people don't realize that we have to use potatoes of different sizes, depending on the size of the bags that we are trying to fill. By grading the potatoes and putting them in these crates, we are able to feed our production lines with the right-sized potatoes. ③

> Ninety percent of Utz chips are eaten within one week of when they are made.

> The main production facility in Hanover, PA, produces between 850,000 and 900,000 bags of potato chips and corn products during each 19-hour production day.

We have potato storage at our factory on Carlisle Street in Hanover and at our High Street facility. The High Street plant has a capability of storing about 40 million pounds of potatoes. We use potatoes from the storage facility to ensure quality as we go through the winter months. The rooms are divided off so that we can keep track of specific farmers, fields, and varieties of potatoes in the various rooms. If some potatoes should start to go bad, we are able to isolate those that may start to deteriorate. The rooms are kept at about 50 degrees and at about 90 to 95 percent humidity. This has the effect of making the potatoes dormant so that there is very little chemical action going on within them. That helps keep them fresh. When we're getting ready to use those potatoes, we have to warm them up and take them out of dormancy. We do that by very slowly raising the temperature in the storage room, usually about one degree a day, until we bring them back. Then we can use them to produce potato chips.

Many people don't realize that potatoes have a lot of moisture in them. And one thing that makes a big difference for us is how much moisture they have versus how much solid material. In order to determine that, we measure the specific gravity of the potatoes. First we determine the weight of the potatoes in a basket in the open air. Having gotten the weight just with the effects of gravity, we then weigh that basket of potatoes in a bucket of water. That tells us the specific gravity of those potatoes. The moisture content of potatoes has a big effect on how long they have to fry and the quality of the chips. ④

Additionally, we inspect the potatoes for disease or damage, and do that by cutting them apart and looking for defects or any signs of disease. And if we find a load of potatoes where there are a significant number of defects, that load will be rejected.

Our primary waste-water treatment operation is located in the basement below the frying room. ⑤ We recover three different streams of waste water in this operation. The first one is the starch operation. We are able to recover about 2.6 million pounds of starch each year and sell it. The second part of the operation recovers the peels from the potatoes as they're being peeled upstairs. All of those potato peels and potato pieces go to animal feed. The third part of our waste-water treatment

operation is an oil and water separator operation, which recovers about 125,000 gallons of oil each year from the water. That oil is then sold to rendering companies to be made into other products. We use our water continuously during a day's production and then we recycle it in our biological batch reactor, which is located behind our facility here on High Street. We are able to clean up that water so it is stream-quality before it's returned to the borough of Hanover.

We're now in the frying room, where the potatoes go into the batch peelers. The peelers have a drum on the inside that's lined with abrasive. The potatoes spin with water in that drum, and the abrasive rubs the peel off. We can adjust the speed and the time that the potatoes are in the peeler so we don't take off more than just the peel, and we save all of the meat of the potato to turn into chips. The inspectors are looking for green spots, dark spots, any sort of bad spot that they can take off the potatoes before they go into the process of becoming chips. ⑥

Salie Utz first produced potato chips in 1921, using hand-operated equipment that could make about 50 pounds of chips per hour. In 1936, the company installed one of the first automatic potato chip cookers, capable of producing 300 pounds per hour.

We're looking at the head of a slicer. The brass ring has surgical steel blades that are mounted on the inside of the ring. They're set at a distance from the side of the ring using a micrometer. This brass ring will then go into the slicer, where it spins. The potatoes are dropped in the center, and, using the surgical steel blades precisely set, we get uniform thickness of slices that are going to become chips. ⑦

These potatoes are being made into regular potato chips. When we are making regular chips, we wash the pieces after the potatoes are sliced. After we've washed the slices, we dry the water off as much as we can before frying. It's these washed slices that give us that starch we talked about recovering during the wastewater treatment operation. Once the slices have been dried as much as possible, they go into the fryer. The fryer has hold-down valves inside, which hold the slices down as they're going through and becoming chips. There are paddles to move the slices along as well as paddles to keep the chips submerged. It takes about 2½ to 3 minutes in the hot oil for these slices to become chips. ⑧

As the chips come out of the fryer, it's our practice to salt them while they're still warm. In the case of Utz chips, we pride ourselves on the fact that we use less salt than most other chip makers, and thereby are able to produce a chip that is much lower in sodium. (9)

As the chips are coming out of the fryer, we have an analyzer that's able to take readings on the moisture and oil content of the chips as they come by.

Additionally, we move these chips through a device that is able to take the dark chips out. It has cameras in it, and those cameras are looking for dark spots. At the front of the machine are tubes, which have compressed air in them. As the cameras detect dark chips, a blast of air is released from the appropriate tube so that it forces that chip off of the conveyor. That's how we are able to remove the dark chips with this machine. After the finished chips come off the line, we move them to the packaging machine.

We're now seeing the packaging room, where our chips have been moved before going into the packaging machines. We have inspectors here, again looking for dark chips and pulling them out. By the way, all of those dark chips go to animal feed. As the good chips come off of the conveyor line toward the packaging machine, we season them just before they go into the bag. (10)

We're looking at our computerized scales. There are queuing buckets at the top of the scales, which take in the product. Then those buckets open up and fill the lower buckets. The computer weighs the chips in the lower buckets, and then opens the right combination of buckets, so that the weight in our bag comes out to within a gram of what it's supposed to be. If we put more product in our bag than is called for, we call that a give-away, because it's something that the consumer doesn't have to pay for. So it makes good business sense for us to try to be as accurate as possible with the amount of weight that we put in our bags. **(11)**

We're now by the packaging machine. Many people don't realize that our bags actually come to us as rolls of film. They start out as flat pieces of paper that we make into bags as part of the packaging operation. As the paper moves through, it is pulled over a form. There is a heating device at the back that forms the back seal of the bag. Then there are jaws, which cut off the bag, sealing the top of the bag that's just been filled, while sealing the bottom of the bag that's next to be filled. As we go through this process, nitrogen is introduced into the bag to push the oxygen out. By eliminating that oxygen, the product stays fresh much longer. As the finished bags come out, they're packed.

Many of the companies in our industry have gone to automated packing machines. We've continued to use packers, which gives us our final quality-control check before the product goes into the box. **(12)**

> Bill and Salie Utz's first chips were sold under the name "Hanover Home Brand Potato Chips."

Central Pennsylvania's Full Service Violin Shop

V OLIN MAKERS LIMITED

Location	Violin Makers Limited
	3300 Rear Market Street
	Camp Hill, PA 17011
	(800) 865-2373
	www.vml123.com
Hours	Public tours available by appointment only.
Tour Guide	Quince Eddens
	President

My name is Quince Eddens and this is Ronald Sachs, my partner, and we represent Violin Makers Limited. Today we're going to show you how we made this violin, and how we make other instruments in this shop. ①

The top wood that we use in this shop all comes from Italy. In Italian spruce, the grain is very even all the way across, and there are approximately 15 lines per inch of grain. We buy this directly from Europe. It comes together in the form of a wedge. We saw it down the center, and then take both of the pieces and glue them together. The two pieces are put against the light to make sure that the joint is perfect all the way up and down, and no light comes through. Now I'm going to go over and glue the joint. ②

The glue we use has the consistency of a syrup. This glue joint is considered to be permanent, so the glue is nice and hot. We brush an even coat onto both sides. I have to work quickly, because the glue really does dry or set very quickly. The glue will cure completely in about 24 hours, but for an initial grab it will be strong enough to go to the next operation in about two hours. We don't want to clamp it too tightly. After the glue joint is totally dry, the top is planed. This will clean off any of the excess glue, and then we can check our glue joints. There shouldn't be any gaps for the whole length of the joint. ③

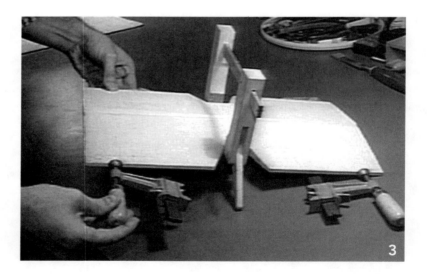

The next step is to make the sides of the violin bend around and give the violin its shape. First we have to construct a mold. A mold is something that is used so that when we are bending the sides, they have something to push against to keep their shape. Every one is different and designed for the exact model of violin that we are going to make. ④

Today we're making a Guarneri violin. There was a man named Giuseppe Guarneri del Gesu who lived in Italy about 350 years ago, and this shape is his model.

This is a modern version of a mold. It's thinner and it's made out of plywood so that it doesn't twist or distort.

We're going to make the six blocks that are in the violin, a couple of which I have already completed.

The basic raw material that we use to make the six blocks, four corner blocks and the top and bottom block, is spruce. This spruce also comes from Italy. The grain is 90 percent straight up, and it's also straight across. The reason we use wood like this is that when we are using chisels, we get a very clean cut straight through. On this piece of wood I'm just going to "true" the side on a sander. The height we want the blocks on this particular violin is approximately 29 millimeters. So using the mold, I'll cut out the block with a band saw. Then I'll sand it to the pattern and check it against the mold to which that piece fits perfectly. What we'll do next is tack the block onto the mold with some temporary glue. ⑤

This piece of metal is a template for drawing the pattern onto the blocks. I'll put that right on top of the block and trace the outline onto the block. Now I'll cut away the excess wood and sand it exactly to this contour. ⑥

We have a piece of maple that is about 1.5 millimeters thick, and now we're going to bend it. We have a bending iron that was made in Germany, and it is extremely hot. We need that heat so that when we're bending the wood it doesn't crack. The heat softens the fiber in the wood, and allows it to bend without cracking. So we're going to bend this to the contour of our mold. And then we will

have the piece that actually glues up against the mold. ⑦

I've just completed bending this rib, which is now going to be glued on the corner block. This is going to fit just like that, and it's the same height as the block. This will curve around, and then it'll be glued onto the bottom block. ⑧

After we've finished gluing all of the sides to the blocks, we want to install a piece of wood that's called the lining. It's a small piece of spruce or willow or linden wood that is bent in the same way that we just bent the ribs using the heat. It goes around the entire inside of the violin and gives strength and rigidity to the whole side or frame assembly. It

also increases the gluing width for the top and the back, which we're going to proceed to next. ⑨

I'm now ready to cut out the actual shape of the violin on the back and the top. This is the back; we'll do that first. We take a template, which is the same model as the violin that we just made the rib structure for, and draw the outline of the violin. We then flip it over and do the same on the other side. Now we have the outline of the violin and we're going to cut it out on the band saw. ⑩

These little pieces of hardened steel in different shapes are called scrapers. They smooth the wood very effectively as they cut. We're using these in place of sandpaper, because unlike sandpaper, the scraper cuts the

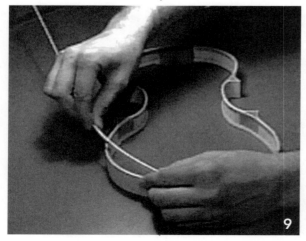

wood and leaves it clean. Sandpaper leaves a lot of dust in the pores of the wood. ⑪

The next step in the violin-making process is to install the base bar. The base bar of an instrument is extremely important to the production of the sound. Inside the violin are two main components. One is the base bar itself, which runs about $10\frac{1}{2}$ inches from one end of the plate to the other. The other component is the sound post. ⑫ Now what I'm going to do is carve this piece of wood so that it fits

perfectly inside the instrument, and then I'm going to pare down its proportions so it responds in an optimum way with the top plate of the instrument. This is the most crucial element to the sound of a violin. There cannot be any gaps down here because you don't want to squeeze the top plate to make it fit to the bar. The bar must sit gently on top of the plate, and fit perfectly. ⑬

Now I've brought the base bar to a pretty good finishing point. It fits perfectly, right along the seam, and that's the way it has to be. The base bar has to be positioned perfectly, and we can't use very much clamping pressure when we're putting a base bar in. As the glue dries, there's a capillary effect that draws the wood together. If we use a clamp and put too much pressure on it, we actually dry the glue joint out by squeezing all the glue out of it. What we want to do is put just enough glue in there to do the job. The idea is not to press the thin, delicate top plate to conform to this rigid bar. We just want to bring the two pieces of wood close together solidly, but not tightly, and then allow them to dry. And what we'll end with is two pieces of wood that have become one. ⑭

The base bar has now been glued in place, and I'm going to start paring it down to a semi-finished configuration. From here I'll start working it much more slowly with a smaller plane and start determining the final shape. There are many different schools of thought on base-barring, but my base bar shapes are determined by the response of the instrument after I play it. So I may take the top off several times and make adjustments on the base bar for each instrument, according to how it's performing. ⑮

The top is now glued onto the sides and to the back, and the entire instrument has been smoothed with scrapers on the top and the back. The F holes are completely finished and carved to the correct size and shape. We removed the clamps, and now we have completed what we call a corpus. The entire body of the instrument is now finished, and all that's left is to carve and install the neck. Then we'll have a completed violin. ⑯

The neck is made out of European maple. We use a template and draw the shape of the neck and the scroll onto the wood. We use an awl and make holes in the maple so we know where to cut our

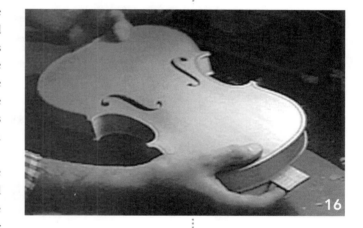

volute. The volute is the twist or turn on the side of the scroll. I'm marking the wood with that shape. ⑰ After the neck is sawed out by the band saw, we have

a rough neck. I'll begin using special gouges and chisels and cut out the shape of the scroll using my original lines to follow the contour of the volute. Using files and other special tools, I'll further refine the shape of the scroll.

The fingerboard is made of ebony. It's solid black throughout. It's a very hard surface and it's what you play the strings on. The fingerboard is glued onto the neck, and then the sides are trimmed. This neck has already been attached to the violin, to

the corpus, and now it is ready to be finished. The entire instrument will be gone over from head to toe to smooth all of the wood down and to make everything perfectly smooth anywhere the player's hands will be. This instrument is now ready for varnishing, which is the final stage. (18)

There are many different steps involved in varnishing. It is a very complicated procedure, and it can take a lifetime to really discover the correct principles of varnishing. The wood has to be sealed before it is ready to receive its first coat of varnish, a clear coat, which has to go on nice and smooth. We don't want to rush this procedure. This violin could take seven to ten coats of varnish. In between each coat there will be a rub-out and color will be added until the final product resembles something similar to this. (19)

WENDELL AUGUST
EST'D 1923

Location	Wendell August Forge 620 Madison Avenue Grove City, PA 16127 (800) 923-4438 www.wendellaugust.com
Hours	Public tours available Monday through Friday, 9:00 a.m. to 12:00 noon, 12:30 p.m. to 4:00 p.m. Showroom open Monday through Thursday and Saturday, 9:00 a.m. to 6:00 p.m.; Friday, 9:00 a.m. to 8:00 p.m.; Sunday, 11:00 a.m. to 5:00 p.m.
Tour Guide	Will Knecht President

The first stop on our tour at Wendell August is probably one of the most interesting artistic processes that you'll see in the state of Pennsylvania. We are blessed to have two of the world's finest hand-engravers who create all of the design work that goes into our products. ① Our two engravers, Dave Bruck and Len Youngo, have been schooled for the last 15 years in an engraving technique that is being lost. There are few engravers today doing the work that Len and Dave do here at Wendell August. And it's interesting to note that the tools they use are the same tools that engravers have been using for centuries, and those are a hammer and a chisel. Our engravers, using that hammer and chisel, engrave into a piece of somewhat softened tool steel. They use various widths of chisels to get wide lines and to get very intricate details.

1

Len will start with a picture done by a local artist. We use western Pennsylvania artists, who will take a concept that comes from our customers and do a pen-and-ink drawing of it. Then the mastery of the engraving begins, coming from the art-work to the chisel and the metal. ②

Our engravers make many of their own tools. Some of the tools that they use have been handed down from the late 19th century. They were made in Germany by some of that country's finest engravers, and they landed in the hands of one of the Franklin Mint's first engravers, Alvin Dehoff. Mr. Dehoff was engraving with the Franklin Mint in the 1960s, and when he retired, he knew that there was only one place that those engraving tools could go. So he gave them to Dave and Len. And they still use some of those engraving tools today. ③

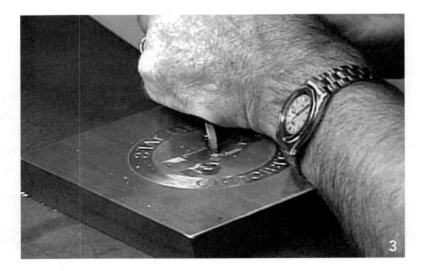

We have about 28 American craftsmen who are still utilizing a technique pio-neered by our founder, Wendell August himself, and that's hand-hammering of metal giftware. Mr. August pioneered that craft in the 1920s. Prior to World War II, we had about 200 competitors, but today we're really the only folks in the world doing what we do, the way we do it.

Our process begins with the cutting of sheet metal. This happens to be aluminum. ④ Once the metal is cut to size, we come to the first step in our hammering process. The die of the design is sitting face-up on the hammering table and Greg Summerville, one of our master craftsmen, is placing the sheet of aluminum on that die. This piece is going to be finished into a waste basket.

Now the hammering begins. Greg is using a specially designed air hammer, guiding it throughout the pattern, and hammering the metal into this chiseled-out portion of the die. He's got to hit each piece and do it in such a sequence that the whole design shows without making any skip in what is created. ⑤

A lot of folks, when they come on tour here, are amazed at how long it can take for one piece to be made. And many of those who buy our products have no idea what goes into them. But those little ripples on the back are individual hammer marks, representing one hit of that hammer.

James McCausland was chief designer for the company for many years. During his tenure, he created designs for Herbert Hoover, Queen Elizabeth II, Henry Ford, John D. Rockefeller, and Mrs. Calvin Coolidge.

During World War II, Mr. August was forced to close his forge, because all major supplies of aluminum were allocated to the War Department for use in weapons manufacturing.

Now Jeff is placing anvil marks, one at a time. He will cover that whole piece of the metal with those marks. One of the things that is said about our products is that no two are ever alike. It's just like a snowflake. You can see, even by what Jeff is doing right now, there's no way that one product can ever be exactly like another. ⑥

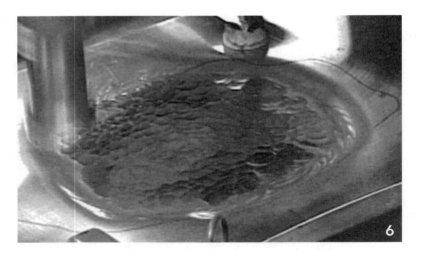

After all of the anviling has been done, Jeff will use a nylon mallet to flatten the piece of metal. It has to be perfectly flat, and in the handcrafting process we use, that's hard to do. Once the piece is absolutely flat, Jeff will begin the process of cutting it to the shape that will be used for the large basket or the waste can.

Here is our namesake—the Wendell August Forge. And basically, it is a big, old coal fireplace. It uses bituminous coal, a very soft coal, that Mark has loaded into the fire. What we'll see here is a billowing fire that just erupts. The whole idea of this is to put a blackening on our design. ⑦

After the death of Wendell August in the early 1960s, his son Robert August ran the company until 1978, when F. W. Knecht III of Youngstown, OH, purchased the forge.

Mark now stokes the fire, getting it to the right temperature, because there is a point at which the metal would melt. So he's got to make sure that the flame is high enough and that the smoke is thick enough that it will bake onto the metal. Mark will hold the metal over the fire. He does not heat the metal, but he bakes the smoke into the design. When it comes out, the black will have attached itself to the metal. This is another signature of Wendell August. As we get more into the polishing stage, we'll see the importance of what Mark has just done.

Next comes a neat stage in the creation of the basket. Jeff is putting it in an old roller sometimes used to dry clothes long ago. He's rolling the metal into its finished shape. So what a few short minutes ago was a flat piece of nondescript metal has now taken the shape of the basket. ⑧

As Jeff hands the piece off to Mark, Mark begins the polishing and the cleaning of our product. He uses a buffing wheel that has been specially designed for us to polish the inside of the can and to polish the areas where the rivets attach the metal.

Then he polishes the outside right around the design, taking off that black smoke that he put on a couple of minutes ago. He'll take it to a different or a less gritty buffing wheel to touch up. Maybe he'll take out a little imperfection he sees in the middle. The amount of pressure that he is able to put on the metal is critical. If he pushes too hard, he can actually burn the metal. If he burns the metal, it will turn a milky white, which will not be good for our product.

Every basket needs a bottom, and we make ours right here, one at a time, putting it in a press. And "voila!" here is the bottom of our large basket. That also is aluminum. ⑨

When we were in the engraving room, we saw that our engravers sign each piece they make. Now Jeff will sign that piece with the Wendell August logo. Jeff Brown is leader of this cell, and his mark goes on each piece that his team creates. So we have the engraver sign it, as well as the company and the craftsman who actually made the piece. A lot of pride and a lot of craftsmanship go into our products.

Jeff is now boring out the holes that connect the bottom. He's going to rivet that bottom in so the two pieces of

Along with its retail business, the company also produces corporate incentive and recognition items for clients such as IBM, H.J. Heinz, Hershey, Walt Disney, and the United States Congress.

metal actually become one. It takes a good touch to work in the little area that Jeff is working in, between the rivet and the bottom. ⑩

The forge used today is one of the originals used in the early 1930s, when the shop was built.

The next step in the process is the fluting of the top. For this step, Jeff is using the nylon mallet. The form he's using is one of the ones we made, possibly in the 1940s. Many things don't change here. We're still doing things the way the giants of our business did 30, 40, or 50 years ago. ⑪

Jeff is making sure that there are no areas in the metal that are even a little bit out of whack. It all needs to be even and consistent throughout. Although it's handmade, we try to make everything very consistent.

You've seen this basket go through the hands of our craftsmen, turning a very nondescript piece of metal into a work of art. This basket is a product we've been making for years, probably since the 1940s. And probably not a month goes by without a guest or a customer coming to visit us here in Grove City and saying, "I can remember getting that as a wedding gift years ago, and we're still using it." That's the durability of the metal, and that's the durability of what these craftsmen do. ⑫

WESTERWALD POTTERY

Location	Westerwald Pottery 40 Pottery Lane Scenery Hill, PA 15360 (724) 945-6000
Hours	Public tours available; groups of ten or more should call first. Gift shop open weekdays, 8:00 a.m. to 5:00 p.m.; Saturday and Sunday, 10:00 a.m. to 5:00 p.m.
Tour Guide	Phil Schaltenbrand President

Westerwald Pottery is located in historic Scenery Hill, PA, about 40 miles south of Pittsburgh. We've been in business here for almost 25 years. The name "Westerwald" comes from a region in Germany famous for its blue and gray stoneware. In fact, it could be said that most of the blue and gray salt-glaze stoneware in the United States today can trace its origins back to the Westerwald region of Germany, perhaps as early as the 1400s. (1)

Eventually, some of those potters came to America. Some of them settled in Pennsylvania, bringing their trade secrets with them, and settling down and establishing potteries here. Many of the stoneware pieces made in America in the 1800s can be traced directly back to the Teutonic antecedents of the German potters.

In the production area, you can see how a piece of pottery is formed on the potter's wheel. Every piece at Westerwald Pottery is thrown on the potter's wheel by hand. A lot of my competitors in recent years have adopted high-tech methods, perhaps special molds or presses to press out a lot of their forms. But at Westerwald we are committed to making pieces entirely by hand. I like the idea of a hands-on approach to working in clay. I have no intention of taking shortcuts or using high-tech mass-production techniques.

Here Grant is wedging and weighing clay. ② This is where the forming process begins. He is taking the moist clay out of the plastic bags as we receive it from the factory, and he is weighing it out in precise amounts. It's very important to have the clay weighed out precisely, because the weight of the clay determines the size of the piece. For example, these look like they're 2½- or maybe 3-pound lumps of clay, and from a lump of clay this size a potter could make about a two-quart container on the potter's wheel.

Grant is also kneading and wedging the clay in his hands. This is being done to make sure that the clay is completely consistent and homogeneous and that there aren't any air pockets, or lumps, or anything that's going to interfere with the throwing process.

In the 1800s, this is how most of the potters started out. They would start as apprentices. This was a testing period to see if they really had the stuff. They would spend maybe a year or two doing nothing but weighing and wedging the clay for a master potter under whom they served. Then, if they had the stuff, they could move up the ladder. Eventually, some of those apprentices turned out to be some of the great potters in the state of Pennsylvania.

Let's move over to the potting area and see how the master's hands will turn a vessel. Sid is throwing a one-quart jar, which is one of the very first types of pieces we ever made at Westerwald Pottery, 25 years ago. It's still one of our best-selling pieces today. He is working with a lump of clay that was laid out by Grant yesterday—$2\frac{1}{2}$ pounds, I believe—to form this particular piece. What Sid is doing looks very simple, but it actually is a very, very difficult process to master. He's been working here for about 10 years, and his hands work almost automatically. But there are years and years of experience in knowing just how much pressure to apply to the clay. ③

At this point, Sid gets his hands down inside the piece, one hand inside and one hand outside. He puts very subtle and gradual pressure from one hand on the outside, pushing against the fingers on the inside. He's able to bring the clay up because it's very plastic and uniform. ④

When he's decided that the piece is shaped correctly, he'll cut the piece with a wire to separate it from the wheel. He'll dry his hands, lift the piece off the wheel, and set it up on his wareboard. In one day a good potter can throw up to 200 pieces.

This is a process that's been done in the identical manner for thousands of years. In fact, the ancient Egyptians threw on a wheel. It wasn't electric, of course, but the wheel was made to spin around very fast by using a foot-powered kick wheel.

Most of the clay that we use at Westerwald is found naturally in the earth in various parts of the eastern United States. There's a stoneware base in this clay that comes from Ohio. But there's also a fireclay that's mixed in to give it more heat resistance, and that comes from Missouri. There's a ballclay, which comes from Tennessee, which makes it easier to throw on the wheel. There are other ingredients worked into the clay to give it a little bit of color. We work with a clay that includes five or six different ingredients.

Most of our handles are made by an extruding machine. They'll come out looking like this—long strips of clay. ⑤ They will be cut into strips of predetermined length and attached to the pitchers, the coffee mugs, and some of the beer steins. This is one of the shortcuts that we take, but it is true to the art form because potters in the 1800s used extruded handles on a lot of their crocks. They are not just more uniform in shape and size, but they can also be made very decorative. We use a ribbing effect that adds a very nice dimension to the pitcher.

5

6

Here we are attaching handles to some coffee cups that were made yesterday. You see the handles that were extruded earlier today. We're blending the handle in, top and bottom, to make sure that it will hold on the side of the piece, and to make sure that it won't crack during the drying stage. Then we clean the piece off, smooth the bottom out, and set it on the board. This piece will dry for the next couple of days, and once it's dry and hard, we won't be able to go back and do any more shaping or cleaning to the piece. It will be finished. ⑥

After the pieces are finished, they are put onto these racks to dry out. Once they're on these racks, they will only be touched three or four more times. The pieces will dry out in the next day or two, and they'll turn into a light gray color called greenware.

Once they are completely dry, they are loaded into the first of the firing kilns, and that will be the bisque kiln. ⑦

The ashes of World War II veterans are buried in Westerwald urns at Arlington National Cemetery.

This is the first of the two firings we do at Westerwald. The first firing will take the pieces up to about 1,600 degrees Fahrenheit. It makes the pieces hard, but not completely impervious to liquid. The pieces can be decorated and finished off, and then they'll go through a second firing. As soon as this kiln is completely loaded, the door will be bricked up, and we'll start the burners. We'll fire this kiln slowly, all afternoon and through the evening, and we'll probably have it finished about this time tomorrow morning. Usually it takes about 16 hours. ⑧

Once the kiln is shut off, it will cool for about 18 hours, and then we'll be able to take all of these bisque-fired pieces back to the decorating department, which is where we're going to go next. We'll see how the pieces are decorated and prepared for glazing, which is the final step in the process.

Westerwald has shipped pottery to its customers on every continent except Antarctica.

Brenda is working on a logo. We're doing some pieces for the Heinz Company. We sometimes make special promotional pieces for large companies. We've been making pottery for Heinz for about 15 years now. This is the Heinz keystone logo with the "57" on it. That will come out a nice, bold dark blue, and then the piece will be trimmed and banded in blue brush strokes. And it will be quite handsome. ⑨

In the past 25 years, Westerwald has stamped the names of more than 12,000 towns and cities into pieces of stoneware.

The company has created special pieces for the Smithsonian, the Boston Museum of Fine Arts, the Henry Ford Museum, the Carnegie Museum, the Chesapeake Maritime Museum, and the Museum of American Culture.

Next we'll see how the pieces are glazed and finished. We work from a large vat of glaze, and we dip the pieces down into the glaze. The glaze is a specially prepared formula. Most of the ingredients produce a glasslike substance when the piece is fired in the kiln. The glass particles on the surface of the vessel will melt and fuse to the pot, and it will cause a colored glaze. ⑩

Westerwald has made custom trophies for many country clubs and golf tournaments. Country clubs include Oakmont, Pebble Beach, Marion Golf Club, and Jupiter Hills.

Gary wipes the bottom of each piece off because we don't want any glaze on the bottom. This glaze will turn to a molten state for about half an hour, and it would stick to the bottom of the kiln.

There are 15 or 16 steps that each piece of pottery goes through here at Westerwald, and we're about to see the last step. That's the glaze-firing. The kiln is the heart of the ceramic operation, and the glaze kiln is the most important of all the firing steps. If anything goes wrong in here, we have to start all over again. ⑪

Grayson and Barry are loading glazed pieces onto the kiln shelves and wiping the bottom of the pieces again to make sure that any glaze on the bottom will be removed. That leaves a very clean surface between the bottom of the piece and the shelf upon which it rests. When they're done loading this kiln, it will probably hold about 700 pots, depending on the size of the piece. Once this kiln is loaded, we will start the burners on low, even heat, and then tomorrow morning, bright and early, we will start blasting the kiln.

When we unload this kiln, all of these pieces will come out and be inspected. We hope they will all be in good condition. They will then be taken up to shipping and sent out to the eager and anxious customers who are waiting for these pots.

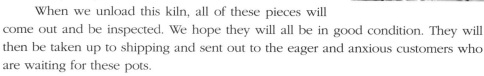

YORK® BARBELL

Location	York Barbell
	3300 Board Road
	York, PA 17402
	(717) 767-6481
	www.yorkbarbell.com
Hours	Public tours of factory not available. Museum open weekdays, 10:00 a.m. to 6:00 p.m.; Saturday, 10:00 a.m. to 5:00 p.m. Free of charge. Retail store open same hours as museum.
Tour Guide	Victor Standish President and CEO

We're standing here in the yard department of U.S. Lock and Hardware Company, a gray iron foundry, which is a wholly owned subsidiary of York Barbell. This is where we make the gray iron castings for York Barbell. I'd like to take you through the steps required to process what you see here, which is cast-iron scrap. We convert radiators and bathtubs into molten iron, then pour it into what we call green sand molds. The sand is the type that you walk on at the beach. ①

The process starts when we take our cast-iron scrap and put it in a furnace, which we call a cupola furnace. It is basically a big tube with a firebrick lining inside. Our combustion agent is coke, which is a byproduct of coal. The coke is put into the furnace, we light it, we induce oxygen and air, and then we pour or dump cast iron on top of the coke. It heats, melts, filters

down through the coke, picking up carbon, and comes out the front of the furnace as molten iron.

What you're seeing here is iron coming out of the front of the cupola furnace. ② We described the combustion agent as coke, and we keep charging iron and coke from 6:00 in the morning till 4:30 in the afternoon. What you see coming out of the front of the furnace here is molten iron at 2,750 degrees.

The molten iron goes into 900-pound bull ladles so we can transfer the iron from the melt department to the molding department. Our bull man next takes that 900-pound bull, loaded with molten iron, using an overhead electrified track system, and delivers the iron to the pour deck. Then we'll transfer the iron into smaller ladles, which will be used to pour the iron into the sand molds.

We're now in the molding department. What you're looking at is a mold being made by our automatic molding machine. ③ We start with an aluminum pattern, which has the impressions of the castings we want to make. This particular pattern has six castings in it, four 10-pound York barbell plates and two 5-pound barbell plates. If you look at the mold, you'll see half of the casting impression here on the bottom, and up underneath is the other half of the casting impression. This machine will blow sand into the boxes with the pattern inside. Then it will open up and pull

the pattern back, as we see here. It will have a hole cut down through the center into which we can pour the iron, which will fill the cavity and create the casting.

We have a 250-ton sand storage system, which distributes sand to our automatic molding machine. We use 400 to 500 tons of sand per day to make our sand molds. The sand is completely recyclable. We put it through a screen and back into the tank for reuse. Our sand needs to be tempered. We put the new sand into our mixing bowl, we add clay to give it strength, we add water and other additives, we mix it, and then we distribute it to our molding machine.

We're now on the pouring deck, and our pourer is pouring the molten iron from the 900-pound bull, or traveling ladle, into the 300-pound pouring ladle. This iron will now be poured directly into the molds to form the castings. At this point, he skims the top, because there are some impurities in the iron that we don't want to get into the mold. ④

York Barbell was founded in 1932 by Bob Hoffman, U.S. Olympic weightlifting coach, who has been honored as the "Father of World Weightlifting."

Our pourers pour the molten iron into the sand molds to create the castings. We have a heavy weight on top of the casting as well as a jacket around the sand mold. When you pour molten iron into a closed cavity, you create a tremendous amount of pressure. We put the jacket and the weight on to keep the two-part mold from splitting or pushing and allowing the iron to flow out. In each mold there could be anywhere from one to a dozen castings, depending on the size and configuration of the casting. These pourers must know how to pour the molds, because every job is different. On some jobs we pour hard or fast; on other jobs we have to pour very slowly. Some jobs require very, very hot iron, and on other ones we have to chill the iron. ⑤

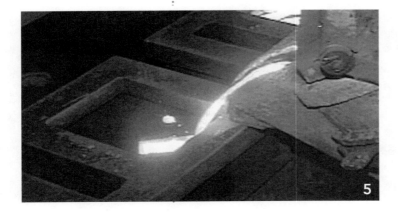

In the shakeout department, all of the castings that were made in the foundry come through a circulating or rotating barrel. The sand from the mold goes down through perforations in the barrel, and the castings are rifled forward onto the vibrating sorting table. You'll see our people down there with their moon hats on. ⑥ That's because we have dry silica in the air, a potential health hazard. Our people will then sort the castings into boxes, but they will not pick them up. Some of those castings could still be red-hot. The castings that are sorted will be placed in tubs and then pushed over into the cooling room, where they'll stay overnight. The next day we will begin the cleaning process.

The Weightlifting Hall of Fame encompasses approximately 8,000 square feet of space and is housed on the first floor of the York Barbell administrative building adjacent to the company's manufacturing facility.

The castings you see here are as they came out of the foundry. ⑦ They still have sand and other particles sticking to them. We clean them with a big machine with perforated steel plates. The castings tumble around inside the machine, and at the same time we're hitting them with hard-steel shot, like BB shot. That takes them from this condition to a clean condition. They're sorted at this point, and any bad castings are thrown out.

York Barbell equipment was used at the Olympic games in 1952, 1968, and 1984, and at the 1999 Pan American games in Winnipeg, Canada.

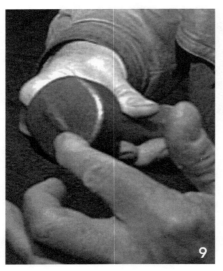

These are clean castings, some of which were cast this morning. We're cleaning them fast today because of the demand. These castings will now be set aside to be finish-ground by our grinding and cleaning department. ⑧

In the final finish operation before inspection, we are grinding any parting lines or imperfections off the end of the casting. This one is a very clean casting, but it still has a parting line on the end where the iron ran into it. ⑨ We're going to clean that off so we have a very, very clean casting. We do this with all our castings. Perhaps that's why our castings cost a little more than the Chinese imports.

Here one of our best grinders is grinding our 20-pound solid dumbbell. ⑩ This is the finest dumbbell made in the world. He is knocking off the rough edges before it goes in for final inspection. These particular dumbbells are then sent over to the main plant of York Barbell, where they're painted, packed, and made ready for shipment. They're so good that we guarantee them for life. You can see how hard these people have to work, and we're very proud of them. They're good American workers.

At the final inspection stage, our inspector looks at every casting. If it needs to be patched, we put a very hard, ironlike

Founder Bob Hoffman served as an official advisor on youth physical fitness for Presidents Eisenhower, Kennedy, and Nixon.

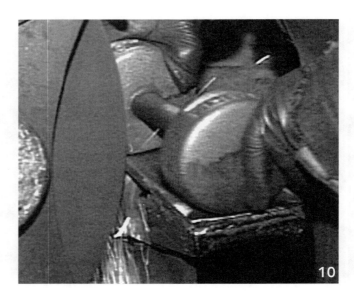

material on it to cover any blemishes, and then we put it in a box to be sent for paint and shipping. ⑪

The castings you see in this skid are now ready to go over to York Barbell, where they will be spray-painted, packaged, and shipped. ⑫ We have the ability to take an order and ship it within five days. That's one of the real benefits that York Barbell has over a lot of the competition. We own our own foundry, we make our own castings, and they're quality castings. This will be good for us for the next 60 years, as it has been for the past 60.

The company published the popular *Strength and Health* magazine from 1932 until 1986. The magazine was recently revived as an online publication through the company's Web site.

To ensure quality control, the York Barbell Company owns its own foundry. Located near the corporate headquarters, the foundry is the oldest continuous producer of dumbbells and barbell plates in the United States.

The company employs 145 people at its 131,550-square-foot plant in York, PA.

Zippo

Location	Zippo Lighters 33 Barbour Street Bradford, PA 16701 (814) 368-2700 www.zippo.com
Hours	No public tour available. Museum open Monday through Saturday, 9:00 a.m. to 5:00 p.m.
Tour Guide	Christine Hannon Assistant to the Vice President of Operations

Zippo is located in the northwest corner of Pennsylvania, just south of the New York state border. We've been in existence for more than 60 years, and we've been in the same location in Bradford, PA, for 60 years. Even though we haven't moved from this location, our distribution has become worldwide. ①

The founder of the company was Mr. George Blaisdell, a Bradford businessman, who was at a dress party one evening, and he was watching a friend try to light

1

a cigarette with a two-piece lighter. He said to the friend, "What, you're all dressed up and here you are with this clumsy lighter." And the friend said, "Well, George, it works." Mr. Blaisdell bought the rights to this lighter and worked it around in such a way that he was able to use the same windproof chimney but made it into a single-piece lighter that could be snapped open with just one hand. With a couple of exceptions, today's Zippo lighter is the same as the original model from 1932. ②

Zippo started out above a filling station in Bradford. The original factory had

three employees and produced about 60 lighters in the first month. Zippo moved to a larger facility in 1944, and in 1956 moved into the present office building.

The click that's so recognizable on a Zippo lighter has been evident in many movies and television shows. This particular model, "The Lady Bradford," used to be a prominent prop in the *I Love Lucy* TV show. It was seen many times sitting on a coffee table when Lucy and Ricky and Fred and Ethel were hatching their plans, and one of them would pick up the lighter. ③

The Zippo lighter received wide recognition during World War II. When America entered the war, Mr. Blaisdell made the decision that all manufacturing would go to the boys on the front. He struck up a friendship with war correspondent Ernie Pyle and sent Mr. Pyle a shipment of lighters. Mr. Blaisdell made the comment in his letter that he was quite sure that Ernie Pyle did not even know what a Zippo lighter was. A short time later in Ernie Pyle's column, he commented that if Mr. Blaisdell only knew how the soldiers coveted the lighter and realized what a popular item it was, he would be amazed. So Mr. Blaisdell began an arrangement with Ernie Pyle to send him shipments of lighters, and Mr. Pyle would distribute them to soldiers.

One of the policies that Mr. Blaisdell instituted in the very beginning was a lifetime guarantee and a promise that "regardless of age or condition, we will never charge a cent for the repair of any Zippo product." This particular lighter was sent to our repair department last year with a note saying, "Dear Sir, A gun went off and if I had not had my Zippo in my shirt pocket, it would have shot me through my chest.

I hope you can fix it." (4) The lighter could not be fixed, so we kept it for our museum. Lighters arrive in all conditions. We get lighters with the hinge broken, or the lid broken off, or needing some minor cosmetic repair, and we gladly repair them and send them back to our customers with a letter thanking them for the opportunity of letting us repair their lighter.

We receive approximately 1,000 lighters a day to be repaired. Zippo repairs the ones that can be fixed and replaces them if they cannot be fixed.

The Zippo factory has become highly automated, although many of our operations are still done by hand. This machine is known as the Waterbury. (5) It takes rolls of coiled brass, feeds them through a series of punches and dies, and brings out the formed top and bottom. They will go down the conveyor belt and through a cleaning system to get ready for the next process.

In addition to lighters, Zippo also manufactures pocket knives, key holders, money clips, writing instruments, tape measures, pocket flashlights, and sport watches.

Between 1934 and 1940, Zippo sold more than 300,000 lighters through the use of punchboard advertising. Considered a game of chance, punchboards were ruled illegal in 1940.

Next is the trimming operation. This is where we take a top to a regular lighter, cut off the excess brass, and put on the hinge notch. As you can see, there's a difference before the operation, on the left, and after the operation, on the right. (6)

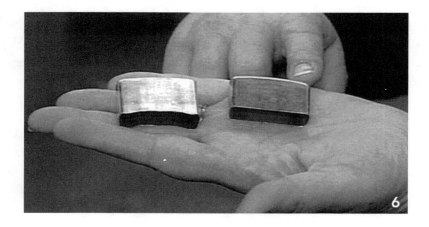

This is the welding operation. ⑦ We have seen the tops made; we have seen the bottoms made. Now we're going to take a top and a bottom and hinge and load them onto the welder, and they're going to travel around the table where they will be welded. Once they're welded, they'll be inspected prior to being sent to the buffing area.

This is the buffing department, where we buff the lighters and get them ready to go to other areas. This is the high-polish buff operation. Using compound and buff wheels, the lighters will be buffed to a high polish. At this point the lighters are again inspected for any defects before they are sent to other areas. ⑧

We also have a hand-buff operation, which we use for our lighters with cases made of precious metals such as sterling silver, 18-karat gold, and any brass product that might have a very delicate pattern.

In the plating department, we do chrome-plating, gold-plating, gold-flashing, and silver-plating. What you're going to see here is the chrome-plate operation in

action. The lighters are loaded onto the racks, and the racks go through a cleaning system and a preparatory system before they are chrome-plated. The lighters, even after they are chrome-plated, are not done yet. Many will now have a design painted on them, and we will see that operation next. ⑨

This is the etching department. What we're doing here is loading a silk screen. ⑩ The silk screens are used to put the patterns onto the lighter. The screen is loaded into the machine, and then a substance known as "resist" will be poured onto the screen and pushed through the screen onto the product. Where the resist is coating the lighter, the case is protected. Where you see the pattern is actually where the acid bath will eat into the lighter, so it can be either paint-filled or just plated over to show what we call a "luster-etch finish."

This is the spotting area, where we are making sure everything that should be blue—that is, protected by resist—is blue, and anything that's not supposed to be blue doesn't have any blue on it. ⑪ As we mentioned, the blue is the protected part, and where there is no blue is where the acid will actually attack the lighter to etch the design on it. After the spotters have inspected these lighters, the lighters will go down to our taping operation, where they are loaded onto boards that are known as the etch boards. We take a protective tape and cover each lighter, so when the lighter goes through the acid etch bath, we will not have any acid leaking down inside the boards, damaging the lighter.

Zippo has produced nearly 350 million windproof lighters since 1933, its first year of production. If laid end to end, they would stretch from New York to Los Angeles 3½ times.

The lighters are then loaded onto a rack and passed through the etching system, where they are given an acid bath. They are cleaned off and moved into a drying area. All that occurs in the enclosed etching system. As they come off the back end, you can see how the acid has eaten down into the case, and this case can now be paint-filled. ⑫

In the paint-fill operation, we put paint into the area that we just saw etched out. The same procedure is used here as it was to prepare the lighter for the etching process. We again use a silk screen, but this time paint has been loaded into that silk screen. For each paint color there is a different screen. If it's a lighter that's going to have six different paints, there will be six different screens. The paint is loaded into the screen, and the squeegee comes across and puts the paint on the lighter. The order will be done one color at a time, loading different screens, loading different paints, and repeating the process until done. ⑬

Zippo lighters have become collectibles, with Zippo collectors' clubs organized in England, Italy, Switzerland, Germany, the Netherlands, Japan, and the United States.

What we're doing here is taking off the excess paint. When the lighter goes through the etching operation and the paint fill is put in, a lot of times the paint bleeds over the sides. In order to enhance the picture and show a clear image, we go through this cleaning process. The lighters are also going through a visual inspection before they go to the area where they will be "fit up," cleaned, and boxed. ⑭

During World War II, due to shortages of brass and chrome, Zippo cases were made of porous steel and painted with a thick, black paint that was baked to a black crackle finish. Zippo's entire production was distributed to Army exchanges and Navy ships' stores.

Zippo produces about 15 million lighters a year. The plant in Bradford produces nearly 70,000 a day.

Zippo was given its name as a derivative of the word *zipper*. Zippo inventor George G. Blaisdell liked the sound of the word *zipper*, a device that had been patented in nearby Meadville, PA.

Here the case that has already gone through the customization area is being fit up with our inside unit, which is also made at Zippo. If the inside unit does not fit the case at first, we make adjustments to the case. After the fit-up procedure, the lighters are again cleaned and inspected. (15)

After the lighters are fit up, the next operation is the final step. Here the lighters are cleaned, labels are put on, they're placed in the box, and the guarantees are enclosed. The lighters then receive their final inspection before going out the door to the customer. (16)

Appendix 1

Complete List of *PCN Tours*

Since *PCN Tours* premiered on April 7, 1995, with a tour of the Harley-Davidson plant in York, PA, the program has featured more than 250 tours of factories, museums, and historic sites. These are the tours that have appeared on PCN:

Manufacturing Sites

All-Clad Cookware
424 Morganza Road,
Canonsburg, PA 15317
(412) 745-8300
http://www.allclad.com/

Allen Organ Company
150 Locust Street, Macungie, PA 18062
(610) 966-2202
http://allenorgan.com/

Andover Industries
RD #2, Dunham Road,
Meadville, PA 16335
(814) 337-2394

ANI-Motion
950 Pembroke Road,
Bethlehem, PA 18017
(610) 954-0900
http://www.animot.com/

Aqua Penn Spring Water
One Aqua Penn Drive,
Milesburg, PA 16853
(814) 355-5556

Asher's Chocolates
80 Wambold Road, Souderton, PA 18964
(800) 438-8882
http://www.ashers.com/

Avanti Cigars
1015 North Main Avenue,
Scranton, PA 18508
(800) 586-8409
http://www.avanticigar.com/

Bansner's Ultimate Rifles
261 East Main Street,
Adamstown, PA 19501
(717) 484-2370
http://www.bansnersrifle.com/

Beistle Party Favors
1 Beistle Plaza, Shippensburg, PA 17257
(717) 532-2131
http://www.beistlemfgrs.com/

Bemis Company, Inc.
20 Jaycee Drive,
West Hazleton, PA 18202
(570) 455-7741
http://www.bemis.com/

Berwick Industries Gift Ribbon
Bomboy Lane and Ninth Street,
Berwick, PA 18603
(570) 752-5934

Boeing
Route 291 and Stewart Avenue,
Ridley Park, PA 19078
(610) 591-2700
http://www.boeing.com/

Borders Books
1981 Fulling Mill Road, Suite 101,
Middletown, PA 17057
(800) 644-7733
http://www.borders.com/

Burley's Ice Rink Supply
195 Jari Drive, Suite 100,
Johnstown, PA 15904
(814) 487-5778
http://www.burleys.com/

Burpee Seeds
300 Park Avenue, Warminster, PA 18974
(215) 674-4900
http://www.burpee.com/

Byers' Choice
4355 County Line Road,
Chalfont, PA 18914
(215) 822-6700
http://www.byerschoice.com/

C.F. Martin & Company
510 Sycamore Street,
Nazareth, PA 18064
(800) 633-2060
http://www.martinguitar.com/

C-COR.net
60 Decibel Road, State College, PA 16801
(814) 238-2461
http://www.c-cor.net/

Carlisle Tire and Rubber
621 North College Street,
Carlisle, PA 17013
(717) 249-1000
http://www.carlisletire.com/

Chaddsford Winery
U.S. Route 1, P.O. Box 229,
Chadds Ford, PA 19317
(610) 388-6221
http://www.chaddsford.com/

Chamberlain Manufacturing
156 Cedar Avenue, Scranton, PA 18505
(570) 342-7801
http://www.cmcscr.org/

Channellock Handtools, Inc.
1306 South Main Street,
Meadville, PA 16335
(800) 724-3018
http://www.channellock.com/

Circle Systems Group
653 Bushkill Street, Easton, PA 18042
(610) 253-3400
http://circlesystemgroup.com/

Colver Power Plant
141 Interpower Drive, Colver, PA 15927
(814) 748-7961

Community Loudspeakers
333 East Fifth Street, Chester, PA 19013
(610) 876-3400
http://www.community.chester.pa.us/

Conrail Railroad Cars
1000 South Juniata Street,
Hollidaysburg, PA 16648
(215) 209-4586
http://www.conrail.com/

Cove Shoes
107 Highland Street,
Martinsburg, PA 16662
(814) 793-3786
http://www.coveshoe.com/

Cunningham Piano
5427 Germantown Avenue,
Philadelphia, PA 19144
(215) 438-3200
http://www.cunninghampiano.com/

Double H Boot Company
30 North Third Street,
Womelsdorf, PA 19567
(800) 233-7141
http://www.doublehboots.com/

Dwight Lewis Lumber Company
30 South Main Street,
Picture Rocks, PA 17762
(800) 233-8450
http://www.lewislp.com/

E.H. Hall/Westfield Tanning
360 Church Street, Westfield, PA 16950
(814) 367-5951
http://www.westan.com/

Easy to Love Wooden Toys
RD #2, Box 436, Tyrone, PA 16686
(814) 742-7407
http://www.ez2love.com/

Eisenhart Wallcoverings
400 Pine Street, Hanover, PA 17331
(717) 632-8024
http://www.eisenwalls.com/

Empire Kosher Poultry
RR #5, Box 228, Mifflintown, PA
(717) 436-5921
http://www.empirekosher.com/

Excel Modular Homes
224 St. Louis Street,
Lewisburg, PA 17837
(717) 444-3395
http://www.excelhomes.com/

Frog, Switch and Manufacturing
600 East High Street, Carlisle, PA 17013
(717) 243-2454
http://www.frogswitch.com/

Fry Communications Printing
800 West Church Road,
Mechanicsburg, PA 17055
(717) 766-0211
http://www.frycomm.com/

G.E. Locomotives
2901 East Lake Road, Erie, PA 16531
(814) 875-3457
http://www.GE.com/transportation/

G.S. Electric
1700 Ritner Highway, Carlisle, PA 17013
(717) 243-4041
http://www.gselectric.com/

Gardners Candies, Inc.
Adams Avenue, Tyrone Industrial Park,
Tyrone, PA 16686
(800) 242-2639
http://www.gardnerscandies.com/

Gene Landon, Cabinetmaker
144 Quaker State Road,
Montoursville, PA 17754
(570) 433-3476

Gertrude Hawk Chocolate
9 Keystone Park, Dunmore, PA 18512
(570) 342-7556
http://www.gertrudehawk.com/

Greenleaf Corporation
1 Greenleaf Drive, Saegertown, PA 16433
(800) 458-1850

Hanover Shoe Farms
Route 194 South, Hanover, PA 17331
(717) 637-8931
http://www.hanoverpa.com/

Harley-Davidson Motorcycles
1425 Eden Road, York, PA 17402
(717) 852-6440
http://www.harley-davidson.com/

Herr's Foods
Routes 1 and 272, Nottingham, PA 19362
(800) 63-SNACK
http://www.herrs.com/

Hershey Brothers Dairy
917 Locust Grove Road,
Manheim, PA 17545
(717) 664-2135
http://users.supernet.com/hershey/

Hershey Foods Corporation
100 Crystal A Drive, Hershey, PA 17033
http://www.hersheys.com/

High Steel Structures, Inc.
1770 Hempstead Road,
Lancaster, PA 17601
(717) 390-4270
http://www.highsteel.com/

Holly Milk
405 Park Drive, Carlisle, PA 17013
(717) 486-7000
http://www.landolakes.com/

ITT Industries Engineered Valves
33 Centerville Road, Lancaster, PA 17603
(717) 509-2416
http://www.engvalves.com/

J.E. Morgan Knitting Mills
RD #2, Route 54 West,
Tamaqua, PA 18252
(570) 668-3330
http://www.j-e-morgan.com/

J & L Specialty Steel
Fourth and Stanwix Streets, 18th Floor,
Pittsburgh, PA 15222
(412) 338-1600
http://www.jlspecialty.com/

James Industries (Slinky Toys)
Beaver Street, Hollidaysburg, PA 16648
(814) 695-5681
http://www.slinkytoys.com/

Just Born
1300 Stefko Boulevard,
Bethlehem, PA 18016
(610) 867-7568
http://www.justborn.com/

Ken Smith Bass Guitars
420 Race Street, Perkasie, PA 18944
(215) 453-8887
http://www.kensmithbasses.com/

Kessler's Meats
1201 Hummel Avenue,
Lemoyne, PA 17043
(800) 382-1328

Kimberly-Clark Paper Company
First Street and Avenue of the States,
Chester, PA 19013
(610) 874-4331
http://www.kimberly-clark.com/

Kingdom Computers
719 Lambs Creek Road,
Mansfield, PA 16933
(800) 488-1122
http://www.kingdomcomputers.com/

Kiwi Brand Shoe Polish
447 Old Swede Road,
Douglassville, PA 19518
(800) 289-5494
http://www.kiwicare.com/

KME Fire Apparatus
One Industrial Complex,
Nesquehoning, PA 18240
(800) 235-3928
http://www.kovatch.com/

Koppel Steel
Sixth and Mount Streets,
Koppel, PA 16136
(724) 843-7100
http://www.koppelsteel.com/

Krehling Counter Tops
1399 Hagy Way, Harrisburg, PA 17110
(717) 232-7936

Kunzler and Company, Inc.
652 Manor Street, Lancaster, PA 17604
(888) 586-0537
http://www.kunzler.com/

Kvaerner Philadelphia Shipyard
4605 South Broad Street,
Philadelphia Naval Business Center,
Philadelphia, PA 19112
(215) 875-2600
http://www.phillyshipyard.com/

LaFarge Cement Plant
5160 Main Street, White Hall, PA 18052
(610) 261-3424
http://www.lafargecorp.com/

Lagos Jewelry
441 North Fifth Street,
Philadelphia, PA 19123
(215) 925-1693
http://www.lagos.com/

Lemoyne Sleeper Mattress Company
57 South Third Street,
Lemoyne, PA 17043
(717) 763-1630
http://www.lemoynesleeper.com/

Lesher, Inc. Marble & Granite
2400 Swatara Creek Road,
Middletown, PA 17057
(717) 944-4431

Linden Apparel
321 South Carlisle Street,
Allentown, PA 18103
(610) 435-8024

Little Wonder Outdoor Power Equipment
1028 Street Road,
Southampton, PA 18966
(215) 357-5110
http://www.littlewonder.com/

Mack Trucks, Inc.
7000 Alburtis Road,
Macungie, PA 18062
(610) 709-3011
http://www.macktrucks.com/

MacNeal Maple Syrup
RR #1, Box 134, Rebersburg, PA 16872
(814) 349-2223

Malmark Bellcraftsmen
Bell Crest Park,
P.O. Box 1200,
Plumsteadville, PA 18949
(215) 766-7200
http://www.malmark.com/

Mannings Hand Weaving School
1132 Green Ridge Road,
East Berlin, PA 17316
(717) 624-2223
http://www.the-mannings.com/

Marblux Countertops
27 West Mohler Church Road,
Ephrata, PA 17522
(717) 738-3044
http://www.worktop.com/

Martin's Potato Chips
5847 Lincoln Highway West,
Thomasville, PA 17364
(717) 792-3565

Maryland & Pennsylvania Railroad
96 South George Street, York, PA 17401
(717) 771-1700
http://www.emonstransportation.com/

**McGowan Center for
Artificial Organ Development**
300 Technology Drive,
Pittsburgh, PA 15219
(412) 383-9970
http://www.upmc.edu/mcgowan/

Mead School & Office Products
Main Street, Alexandria, PA 16611
(814) 669-9908
http://www.mead.com/

Middletown & Hummelstown Railroad
136 Brown Street, Middletown, PA 17057
(717) 944-4435
http://www.800padutch.com/mhrr.html

Mine Safety Appliances Company
3880 Meadowbrook Road,
Murrysville, PA 15668
(412) 967-3000
http://www.msanet.com/

Mitterling Butterfly Farm
RD #3, Box 432, Lewisburg, PA 17837
(570) 568-1898

Mrs. T's Pierogies
600 East Center Street,
Shenandoah, PA 17976
(800) 233-3170
http://www.pierogy.com/

New Standard Corporation
74 Commerce Way, York, PA 17406
(717) 757-9450
http://www.newstandard.com/

Nissley Vineyards
140 Vintage Drive, Bainbridge, PA 17502
(800) 522-2387
http://www.nissleywine.com/

Norfolk Southern Conway Freight Yard
2260 Butler Pike,
Plymouth Meeting, PA 19462
(610) 561-3377

Olde Country Reproductions
722 West Market Street, York, PA 17405
(717) 848-1859
http://members.aol.com/pewtarex/

Orthey Instruments
18 Burd Road, Newport, PA 17074
(717) 567-6406
http://www.fmp.com/orthey/

P.H. Glatfelter Paper Company
228 South Main Street,
Spring Grove, PA 17362
(717) 255-4711
http://www.glatfelter.com/

Pacific Coast Pillow Factory
1525 Joel Drive, Lebanon, PA 17042
(717) 228-1950
http://www.pacificcoast.com/

Penn Iron Works
700 Old Fritztown Road,
Sinking Spring, PA 19608
(610) 777-7656
http://www.penniron.com/

Penn State Creamery
12 Borland Lane,
University Park, PA 16802
(814) 865-7535
http://www.cas.psu.edu/docs/CASDEPT/
FOOD/creamery.html

Pennsylvania House
137 North 10th Street,
Lewisburg, PA 17837
(570) 523-1285
http://www.pennsylvaniahouse.com/

Pennsylvania Precision Cast Parts
521 North Third Avenue,
Lebanon, PA 17042
(717) 273-3338
http://www.ppcpinc.com/

The Pfaltzgraff Company
140 East Market Street, York, PA 17401
(717) 848-5500
http://www.pfaltzgraff.com/

Philadelphia Toboggan Roller Coasters
Eighth and Maple Streets,
Lansdale, PA 19446
(215) 362-4700

Phillips Mushroom Farms
1011 Kaolin Road,
Kennett Square, PA 19348
(610) 925-0520
http://phillipsmushroomfarms.com/

Pittsburgh Brewing Company
3340 Liberty Avenue,
Pittsburgh, PA 15201
(412) 692-1191

Quebecor World
South Route 924, Humboldt Industrial
Park, Hazleton, PA 18201
(570) 459-5700
http://www.quebecor.com/

Reynoldsville Casket Company
P.O. Box 68, Fifth Street Extension,
Reynoldsville, PA 15851
(800) 441-8224
http://www.reynoldsvillecasket.com/

Rodale Institute Experimental Farms
611 Siegfriedale Road,
Kutztown, PA 19530
(610) 683-6009
http://www.rodaleinstitute.org/

Sarris Candies
511 Adams Avenue,
Canonsburg, PA 15317
(724) 745-4042
http://www.sarriscandies.com/

Sauder's Eggs
570 Furnace Hill Pike,
Lititz, PA 17543-0427
(717) 626-2074
http://saudereggs.com/

Saylor Cement Plant
245 North Second Street,
Coplay, PA 18037
(610) 435-4664
http://www.voicenet.com/~lchs/
museum/sites/p_say.html

Schulmerich Bells
Carillon Hill, Sellersville, PA 18960
(800) 772-3557
http://www.schulmerichbells.com/

Scranton Lace Company
1313 Meylert Avenue,
Scranton, PA 18509
(800) 822-1036
http://www.scrantonlace.com/

Sears Iron Works
267 Beaver Run Road,
Ottsville, PA 18942
(610) 847-2222

Seldom Seen Coal Mine
P.O. Box 83, Patton, PA 16663
(800) 237-8590

Seltzer's Lebanon Bologna
230 North College Street,
Palmyra, PA 17078
(717) 838-6336
http://www.seltzerslebanonbologna.com/

Signature Door Company
401 Juniata Street, Altoona, PA 16602
(800) 741-2265
http://www.signaturedoor.com/

Silly Putty
1100 Church Lane, Easton, PA 18044
(800) 272-9652
http://www.sillyputty.com/

Sound Technology Ultrasound Probes
1401 South Atherton Street,
State College, PA 16001
(814) 234-4377
http://www.sti-ultrasound.com/

Story & Clark Pianos
269 Quaker Drive, Seneca, PA 16346
(814) 676-6683
www.storyandclark.com/

Straub Brewery
303 Sorg Street, St. Marys, PA 15857
(814) 834-2875
http://www.straubbeer.com/

Sturgis Pretzels
219 East Main Street, Lititz, PA 17543
(717) 626-4354
http://www.sturgispretzel.com/

Sunline Coach Company
245 South Muddy Creek Road,
Denver, PA 17517
(888) 478-6546
http://www.sunlinerv.com/

Sunoco Refinery
10 Penn Center, 1801 Market Street,
Philadelphia, PA 19103
(215) 977-3000
http://www.sunocoinc.com/

Susquehanna Aquaculture Fish Farm
York Haven, PA 17370
(717) 266-4577

Tastykake
2801 Hunting Park Avenue,
Philadelphia, PA 19129
(800) 321-2314
http://www.tastykake.com/

Taylor-Wharton Gas Cylinders
4718 Old Gettysburg Road, Suite 300,
Mechanicsburg, PA 17055
(717) 763-5096
http://www.harsco.com/

Three Mile Island Nuclear Station
Route 441 South, Middletown, PA 17057
(717) 948-8821
http://www.gpu.com/

True Temper Hardware
465 Railroad Avenue,
Camp Hill, PA 17001
(717) 730-3032

United Defense
P.O. Box 15512, York, PA 17405
(717) 225-8000
http://www.udlp.com/

Utz Quality Foods
900 High Street, Hanover, PA 17331
(800) 367-7629
http://www.utzsnacks.com/

Verdelli Fruits and Vegetables
P.O. Box 4920, Harrisburg, PA 17111
(800) 422-8344
http://www.verdelli.com/

Violin Makers Limited
3300 Rear Market Street,
Camp Hill, PA 17011
(800) 865-2373
www.vml123.com/

Water Street Bindery
28 North Water Street,
Lancaster, PA 17603
(717) 293-1310

Weaver Memorials
213 West Main Street,
New Holland, PA 17557
(717) 354-4329

Weaver Model Trains
RR #1, Route 11,
Northumberland, PA 17857
(570) 473-9434
http://www.weavermodels.com/

Wendell August Forge
620 Madison Avenue,
Grove City, PA 16127
(800) 923-4438
http://www.wendellaugust.com/

Wert Bookbinding
9975 Allentown Boulevard,
Grantville, PA 17028
(800) 344-9378
http://www.wertbookbinding.com/

Westerwald Pottery
40 Pottery Lane, Scenery Hill, PA 15360
(724) 945-6000

Willet Stained Glass
10 East Moreland Avenue,
Philadelphia, PA 19118
(215) 247-5721
http://www.willetglass.com/

Williamsport Wirerope Works
P.O. Box 3188, Williamsport, PA 17701
(800) 541-7673
http://www.wwwrope.com/

Woolrich Clothing
1 Mill Street, Woolrich, PA 17779
(800) 995-1299
http://www.woolrich.com/

York Barbell
3300 Board Road, York, PA 17402
(717) 767-6481
http://www.yorkbarbell.com/

York International
631 South Richland Avenue,
York, PA 17402
(717) 771-7890

Youghiogheny Opalescent Glass Company
900 West Crawford Street,
Connellsville, PA 15425
(412) 628-3000
http://www.stainedglassbiz.com/

Yuasa-Exide Batteries
2366 Bernville Road,
Laureldale, PA 19605
(610) 208-1802
http://www.yuasainc.com/

Yuengling Brewery
Fifth and Mahantongo Streets,
Pottsville, PA 17901
(570) 662-4141
http://www.yuengling.com/

Zambelli Fireworks
20 South Mercer Street,
New Castle, PA 16101
(724) 658-6611
http://www.zambellifireworks.com/

Zippo Lighters
33 Barbour Street, Bradford, PA 16701
(814) 368-2700
http://www.zippo.com/

Museums and Historic Sites

Academy of Music
260 South Broad Street, 16th Floor,
Philadelphia, PA 19102
(215) 893-1900
http://www.philorch.org/

Academy of Natural Sciences
1900 Benjamin Franklin Parkway,
Philadelphia, PA 19103
(215) 299-1000
http://www.acnatsci.org/

Altoona Railroad Museum
1300 Ninth Avenue, Altoona, PA 16602
(888) 425-8666
http://www.railroadcity.com/

American Helicopter Museum
1220 American Boulevard, Brandywine
Airport, West Chester, PA 19380
(610) 436-9600
http://helicoptermuseum.org/

American Swedish Historical Museum
1900 Pattison Avenue,
Philadelphia, PA 19145
(215) 389-7701
http://www.americanswedish.org/

Andy Warhol Museum
112 Sandusky Street,
Pittsburgh, PA 15212
(412) 237-8354
http://www.warhol.org/

Betsy Ross House
239 Arch Street, Philadelphia, PA 19106
(215) 627-5343
http://www.ushistory.org/betsy/flaghome.
html

Boyertown Museum of Historical Vehicles
28 Warrick Street, Boyertown, PA 19512
(610) 367-2090

Carnegie Museum Dinosaur Hall
4400 Forbes Avenue,
Pittsburgh, PA 15213
(412) 622-3131
http://www.einpgh.org/cmnh/

Christ Church Cemetery
313 Walnut Street,
Philadelphia, PA 19106

Civil War Library and Museum
1805 Pine Street, Philadelphia, PA 19103
(215) 735-8196

Coolspring Power Museum
P.O. Box 19, Route 19,
Cool Spring, PA 15730
(814) 849-6883

Eastern State Penitentiary
22nd Street and Fairmount Avenue,
Philadelphia, PA 19130
(215) 236-7236
http://www.easternstate.com/

Eckley Miners' Village
RR #2, Box 236, Weatherly, PA 18255
(570) 636-2070
http://sites.state.pa.us/PA_Exec/Historical
_Museum/BHSM/toh/eckley/eckley.htm

Edgar Allan Poe House
532 North Seventh Street,
Philadelphia, PA 19123
(215) 597-8780
http://www.nps.gov/edal/index1.html

Eisenhower Farm
97 Taneytown Road,
Gettysburg, PA 17325
(717) 338-9114
http://www.nps.gov/eise/

Fire Museum of Greater Harrisburg
1820 North Fourth Street,
Harrisburg, PA 17102
(717) 232-8915
http://members.aol.com/JCW37/
FRmuseum.html

Flagship Niagara
150 East Front Street, Erie, PA 16507
(814) 452-2744
http://www.brigniagara.org/

Frank and Sylvia Pasquerilla Heritage Discovery Center
201 Sixth Avenue, Johnstown, PA 15906
(888) 222-1889
http://www.jaha.com/

Frost Entomological Museum
501 ASI Building,
University Park, PA 16802
(814) 863-2865

Gettysburg National Military Park
97 Taneytown Road,
Gettysburg, PA 17325
(717) 334-1124
http://www.nps.gov/gett/

Ghosts of Gettysburg
271 Baltimore Street,
Gettysburg, PA 17325
(717) 337-0445

Ghosts of Pennsylvania
P.O. Box 8134, Reading, PA 19603
(610) 779-8173

Haines Mill Museum
Mill and Dorney Park Roads,
Allentown, PA 18105
(610) 435-4664

Harris/Cameron Mansion
219 South Front Street, Harrisburg, PA
17104   (717) 233-3462
http://www.visithhc.com/harrismn.html

Historical Society of Berks County
940 Centre Avenue, Reading, PA 19601
(610) 375-4375
http://www.berksweb.com/

Jimmy Stewart Museum
845 Philadelphia Street,
Indiana, PA 15701
(800) 83-JIMMY
http://www.jimmy.org/

Johnstown Flood Museum
304 Washington Street,
Johnstown, PA 15901
(814) 539-1889
http://www.ctcnet.net/jaha/

Lehigh County Museum
Hamilton and Fifth Streets,
Allentown, PA 18105
(610) 435-4664
http://www.voicenet.com/~lchs/museum/

Liberty Bell Tour
313 Walnut Street,
Philadelphia, PA 19106
(215) 597-8974
http://www.nps.gov/inde/

Little League Museum
Route 15 South, Williamsport, PA 17701
(570) 326-3607
http://www.littleleague.org/

Lock Ridge Furnace Museum
525 Franklin Street, Alburtis, PA 18011
(610) 435-4664
http://www.voicenet.com/~lchs/museum/
lchsmus.html

Longwood Gardens
Route 1 South,
Kennett Square, PA 19348
(610) 388-1000
http://www.longwoodgardens.org/

Mid-Atlantic Air Museum
11 Museum Drive, Reading, PA 19605
(610) 372-7333
http://www.maam.org/

Mifflinburg Buggy Museum
523 Green Street, Mifflinburg, PA 17844
(570) 966-1355
http://www.lycoming.org/buggy/

Moravian Museum
66 West Church Street,
Bethlehem, PA 18018
(610) 867-0173
http://www.moravianmuseum.org/

Mummers Museum
1100 South Second Street,
Philadelphia, PA 19147
(215) 336-3050
http://www.mummers.com/

Museum of Anthracite Mining
17th and Pine Streets, Ashland, PA 17921
(570) 875-4708
http://sites.state.pa.us/PA_Exec/Historical
_Museum/BHSM/toh/anthmining/
anthracite.htm

Museum of Modern Art Celeste Bartos Film Preservation Center
Salem Route 367, Sawmill Road,
Hamlin, PA 18427
(570) 689-2226
http://www.moma.org/

National Aviary
Allegheny Commons West,
Pittsburgh, PA 15212
(412) 323-7235
http://www.nationalaviary.org/

National Civil War Museum
1 Lincoln Circle at Reservoir Park,
Harrisburg, PA 17103
(800) 258-4729
http://www.nationalcivilwarmuseum.com/

National Watch and Clock Museum
514 Poplar Street, Columbia, PA 17512
(717) 684-8261
http://www.nawcc.org/museum/nawcc/
nawmus.htm

Pennsylvania Anthracite and Heritage Museum
Bald Mountain Road, Scranton, PA 18504
(570) 963-4804
http://sites.state.pa.us/PA_Exec/Historical
_Museum/BHSM/toh/anthheritage/
anthraciteheritage.htm

Pennsylvania Military Museum
Route 322, Boalsburg, PA 16827
(814) 466-6263
http://www.psu.edu/dept/aerospace/
museum/

Pennsylvania Railroad Museum
300 Gap Road, Route 741,
Strasburg, PA 17579
(717) 687-8628
http://www.rrmuseumpa.org/

Pennsylvania State Archives
Third and Forster Streets,
Harrisburg, PA 17108
(717) 783-3281
http://statemuseumpa.org/

Pennsylvania State Museum
Third and North Streets, Harrisburg, PA
17108 (717) 787-4979
http://statemuseumpa.org/

Pennsylvania Trolley Museum
1 Museum Road, Washington, PA 15301
(724) 228-9256
http://www.pa-trolley.org/

Philadelphia City Hall
Philadelphia, PA 19107
(215) 686-2840

Philadelphia Historic Tour
(800) 76-HISTORY
http://www.libertynet.com/

President James Buchanan Memorabilia
P.O. Box 1026, Harrisburg, PA 17108
(717) 783-9882

President James Buchanan Wheatland Mansion
1120 Marietta Avenue,
Lancaster, PA 17603
(717) 392-8721
http://www.wheatland.org/

Quilt Collection (Pennsylvania State Museum)
Third and North Streets,
Harrisburg, PA 17108
(717) 787-4979
http://www.statemuseumpa.org/

Rodin Museum
26th Street and the Parkway,
Philadelphia, PA 19101
(215) 684-7614

Southern Alleghenies Museum of Art
Saint Francis College Mall, P.O. Box 9,
Loretto, PA 15940
(814) 472-3920
http://sama-sfc.org/

Steamtown
150 South Washington Avenue,
Scranton, PA 18503
(888) 693-9391
http://www.nps.gov/stea/

Swigart Antique Auto Museum
514 Penn Street, Huntingdon, PA 16652
(814) 643-0885
http://www.swigartmuseum.com/

Troxel-Steckel House and Farm Museum
4229 Reliance Street, Egypt, PA
(610) 435-4664
http://www.voicenet.com/~lchs/museum/lchsmus.html

USS Olympia
211 South Columbus Boulevard,
Philadelphia, PA 19106
(215) 925-5439

Valley Forge National Historical Park
Route 23 and North Gulph Road,
King of Prussia, PA 19406
(610) 783-1000

William Penn Treaty Collection
P.O. Box 1026, Harrisburg, PA 17108
(717) 783-9882
http://www.statemuseumpa.org/

York County Fire Museum
757 West Market Street, York, PA 17404
(717) 783-0464

Other *PCN Tours*

AccuWeather
385 Science Park Road,
State College, PA 16903
(814) 237-0309
http://www.accuweather.com/

AT&T Broadband Communications
300 Corliss Street, Pittsburgh, PA 15220
(412) 771-8100
http://www.broadband.att.com/

Fort Indiantown Gap
Annville, PA 17003
(717) 861-8720
http://dmva.state.pa.us/

Hersheypark
100 West Hersheypark Drive,
Hershey, PA 17033
(800) 437-7439
http://www.hersheypa.com/

Laurel Hill Cemetery Company
3822 Ridge Avenue,
Philadelphia, PA 19132
(215) 228-8200

National Weather Service
227 West Beaver Avenue,
State College, PA 16801
(814) 234-9412
http://www.nws.noaa.gov/er/ctp

Nazareth Speedway Driving School
P.O. Box 221, Blakeslee, PA 18610
(800) RACE-NOW
http://www.racenow.com/

Pennsylvania Emergency Management Agency (PEMA)
2605 Interstate Drive,
Harrisburg, PA 17106
(717) 651-2001
http://www.pema.state.pa.us/

Pennsylvania State Police Academy
175 East Hersheypark Drive,
Hershey, PA 17033
(717) 533-9111

Pennsylvania Tax Return Processing
1131 Strawberry Square,
Harrisburg, PA 17128
(717) 787-8201
http://www.psp.state.pa.us/

QVC Network
1200 Wilson Drive,
West Chester, PA 19380
(610) 701-1000
http://www.iqvc.com/

Solid Waste Landfill
RD #4, Schultz Road, Pine Grove, PA 17963
(570) 345-2777

U.S. Postal Service
1425 Crooked Hill Road,
Harrisburg, PA 17107
(202) 268-2155
http://www.usps.com/

W.B. Saul High School of Agricultural Sciences
7100 Henry Avenue, Philadelphia, PA 19128
(215) 487-4467

Gettysburg Battlefield Tours

On July 1, 2, and 3 of each year, the anniversary dates of the Battle of Gettysburg, the National Park Service offers walking tours of the significant sites of the battlefield. These tours, conducted by Gettysburg National Military Park rangers, are each approximately two hours in length. PCN has been providing full coverage of these tours every year since 1996.

Day One

McPherson's Ridge
The Union 11th Corps
Attack of Brigadier General Daniel's Brigade
Confederate Attack on Seminary Ridge
147th New York Infantry and 2nd Maine Battery
Brigadier General John Buford's Cavalry Division
Brigadier General Roy Stone's Brigade
Union Retreat through Gettysburg
General Lee's Approach from Cashtown
The Attack and Defense of Oak Ridge
Confederates Attack on Blocher Knoll and the Union Right

Day Two

Culp's Hill
The Peach Orchard
General Barksdale's Assault
Little Round Top
General Longstreet's Counter-March
Major General Richard Anderson's Division
Major General Robert Rodes and Cemetery Hill
Brigadier General Caldwell in the Wheatfield
Brigadier General Barksdale's Mississippi Brigade at Gettysburg
Sacrifice of the 1st Minnesota Infantry
Devil's Den, 1863 to the Present
Colonel George Lamb Willard's Brigade

Day Three

The Artillery
Pickett's Charge
Pettigrew's Charge—Union Perspective
Pickett's Charge—Pettigrew's Perspective
Brigadier General George Armstrong Custer's Brigade
The Attack and Repulse of Kemper's Brigade
Farmsteads of Pickett's Charge
Clash at East Cavalry Field
Farnsworth's Charge
Attack and Repulse of Longstreet's Assault

Other Gettysburg Tours

Children's Program
National Cemetery
Burial of the Unknown Soldier
General Longstreet's Monument Dedication
The Wounded and the Dead
Gettysburg Before the War

Purchasing Videotapes of *PCN Tours*

Videotape copies of *PCN Tours* are available for $29.95 including tax and shipping, regardless of the length of the program. Individuals are requested to pay in advance by check to:

Pennsylvania Cable Network
401 Fallowfield Road
Camp Hill, PA 17011

Or call PCN at (717) 730-6000.

Institutions may be invoiced.

Educators are welcome to record *PCN Tours* for use in the classroom free of charge.

PCN Tours on TV

The television series on which this book is based continues to run on the Pennsylvania Cable Network. New episodes air every Sunday evening at 8:00 p.m. "Classic" tours such as those found in this book are aired Monday through Friday at 7:00 a.m. and 5:00 p.m.

A schedule of upcoming *PCN Tours* can be found on PCN's Web site at www.pcntv.com.

Appendix 2

About PCN

The Pennsylvania Cable Network is a nonprofit, nonpartisan cable television network responsive to the interests and needs of Pennsylvania and its people.

The commonwealth's version of C-SPAN, PCN delivers unedited live and same-day coverage of Pennsylvania Senate and House floor proceedings, committee hearings, press conferences, speeches, and other public forums where the business of the state is debated, discussed, and decided. State government coverage on PCN is shown without commentary or analysis, giving viewers the opportunity to judge for themselves the merit of pending bills and the ideas and opinions of state leaders.

PCN also televises extensive coverage of significant state events, such as the Pennsylvania State Farm Show and high school sports championships. Additional network offerings include visits to museums and manufacturing facilities in the commonwealth, interviews with authors of books about Pennsylvania, and hour-long profiles of prominent state residents.

Pennsylvania cable television companies fund and voluntarily carry PCN on their channel lineups. The network receives no state or federal funds.

PCN History

Origins

PCN was organized in 1979 as a nonprofit corporation by 11 Pennsylvania cable companies. Its original purpose was to provide a cable television network for the distribution of educational programming from Pennsylvania institutions of higher learning under the leadership of The Pennsylvania State University.

PCN marked the first use of cable technology for distance learning, and was founded as the first educational cable television network in the nation.

Educational programming on PCN was composed of college courses for credit, literacy-training programs, and general-enrichment shows. These programs were organized by Penn State on behalf of participating state institutions of higher learning, including the University of Pittsburgh, Bloomsburg University of Pennsylvania, Indiana University of Pennsylvania, and several community colleges.

Development of a Network

Until 1994, the interconnection of cable systems for the educational network was through a 796-mile microwave system. PCN programming was passed along under a shared-cost arrangement.

With initiatives undertaken in early 1993, PCN began distributing its signal using compressed-digital satellite technology. The new PCN delivery system—one of the first utilizations of compression technology for a cable network—made the programming signal available throughout Pennsylvania and reduced both the cost and the lead time needed for cable companies to receive the signal.

Public Affairs Programming

Concomitant with its technical initiatives in the early 1990s, PCN expanded its programming format to include nonpartisan public affairs coverage. The new programming began with coverage of "Capitol for a Day" town meetings in 1992 and continued with the establishment of a Tuesday- and Thursday-night public affairs programming block in August 1993. Less than two years later, PCN was televising daily coverage of the state General Assembly as the "C-SPAN of Pennsylvania."

While live and unedited coverage of legislative activities and events is the focus of PCN public affairs programming, the network also televises events that showcase Pennsylvania business, history, culture, and people. PCN has carried the Pennsylvania State Farm Show and Battle of Gettysburg anniversary events since 1995 and has aired walking tours of hundreds of manufacturing facilities in the commonwealth, such as those featured in this book.

Status Today

In August 1996, PCN ended its seventeen-year relationship with Penn State and assumed full responsibility for all programming and operations of the 24-hour-a-day network.

Today, PCN serves nearly three million Pennsylvania households. The network is available on 140 cable systems—more than four times the number of systems that carried the nonprofit service prior to its satellite delivery and public affairs programming initiatives. PCN remains funded through a monthly fee paid by participating cable companies to cover network capital and operating costs and receives no tax dollars.

PCN is now recognized as the preeminent state public affairs network in the nation and is one of the largest regional cable television news organizations in America. Among its many programming milestones, PCN is credited with the first live coverage of a hearing held by the Pennsylvania House of Representatives, the first telecast of a Pennsylvania appellate court hearing, the most extensive coverage of a state election in television history, and the first statewide telecast of a regular-season Pennsylvania high school sporting event.

PCN Program Descriptions

Pennsylvania General Assembly

Floor proceedings of the Pennsylvania Senate and House of Representatives are generally carried on a live or same-day basis on PCN and are always shown gavel-to-gavel. In addition, Senate and House committee hearings, news conferences, and speeches are covered in their entirety, providing viewers with a comprehensive look at the legislative process.

The Executive Branch

PCN covers public activities of the governor, such as speeches, press conferences, and bill-signing ceremonies—all unedited and uninterrupted. Meetings and other forums held by state agencies such as the Departments of Agriculture, Education, Labor and Industry, and Transportation are also televised, giving Pennsylvanians a better understanding of the inner workings of their state government.

The Judicial Branch

Although the Pennsylvania Supreme Court does not permit television coverage, PCN does air *en banc* sessions of the state Superior Court. The Superior Court was created by the Pennsylvania General Assembly in 1895 to ease the burden of the Supreme Court, thus giving the commonwealth two appellate courts with separate jurisdictions.

Business and Industry

Coverage of business in the commonwealth includes industry- and trade-association conferences and conventions, labor union conferences, business roundtables, luncheon speeches, award ceremonies, and news conferences.

The Media

The media itself plays an ever-increasing role in the democratic process. To help viewers gain insight into this aspect of the political debate, PCN devotes time to coverage of activities of Pennsylvania's news and information providers, including television, radio, cable television, newspapers, and computer services. The network also televises editorial board meetings and talk radio shows and produces a monthly program in which state capital correspondents converse on issues of the day.

Culture and History

PCN covers events that reflect the communities, history, and culture of the state. These may consist of tours of historic sites; lectures on aspects of the state's history; high school and college music, academic, and sports competitions; and coverage of community and ethnic festivals.

PCN Series Descriptions

PCN Tours

As part of its coverage of state business and industry, PCN tours museums and manufacturing facilities in the commonwealth. Originally a weekly series, *PCN Tours* now airs weekdays at 7:00 a.m. and 5:00 p.m., in addition to a Sunday-night premiere showing at 8:00 p.m. All video visits are led by a representative of the toured facility and are televised with a minimum of edits. Suggestions for museum or plant tours are always welcome; PCN does not receive payment for producing a walking tour.

PA Books

PCN president Brian Lockman interviews authors of books about Pennsylvania on *PA Books*. The one-hour program features writers and editors of new or recent books touching upon state history, events, industry, people, and culture. New programs air Sundays at 9:00 p.m. and are replayed the following day at 11:00 a.m. Interviews from PCN's extensive library of *PA Books* are presented on weekdays at 8:00 a.m.

PCN Profiles

Hour-long conversations with prominent state residents are shown weekly on *PCN Profiles*. The series airs Sundays at 10:00 p.m., with a second showing the next day at 10:00 a.m. The program is less issue-oriented than other public affairs offerings on PCN, tending toward life and career decisions made by the show's guests that shaped their personal development.

PCN Call-in Program

PCN's live call-in program, which allows viewers to speak directly with elected officials, newsmakers, and other knowledgeable parties on current commonwealth issues, is televised on Mondays and Thursdays from 7:00 p.m. to 8:00 p.m.

Homework Help on PCN

Televised during the school year, *Homework Help on PCN* makes state-certified math and science teachers available to assist primary- and secondary-school students with scholastic assignments. There is no charge for the phone call to the program, nor for the instructional assistance. The live program airs Sundays from 5:00 p.m. to 7:00 p.m.

PCN Game of the Week

Recognizing the strong tradition of scholastic athletics in Pennsylvania, PCN carries a regular-season high school football game on Friday evenings during the autumn months. Games—chosen from across the state—air live on PCN at 7:00 p.m. and are replayed on Saturdays at 11:00 p.m.

Journalists Roundtable

Every month, PCN produces a program with members of the media who cover state legislative activities. The resulting one-hour program, *Journalists Roundtable*, is a candid review of pending state bills and issues, and a forecast of trends and developing concerns. It airs the last Thursday of the month at 8:00 p.m.

Pennsylvania Press Club

The Pennsylvania Press Club meets one Monday each month at the Tuesday Club in downtown Harrisburg. Invited speakers make opening remarks and respond to questions posed by members of the media and other Press Club attendees. The luncheons are open to the public. PCN traditionally airs *Pennsylvania Press Club* coverage the same night at 7:00 p.m.

First Thursday

A monthly debate series organized by Penn State–Harrisburg, *First Thursday* brings together two opposing state legislators or political pundits on a specific state issue. The program takes place on the first Thursday of the month at the Pennsylvania Cable & Telecommunications Association building on State Street in Harrisburg and is open to the public. PCN airs coverage of the debate later the same day.